POETRY NOW
NORTHERN IRELAND,
SCOTLAND & WALES 2003

Edited by

Kelly Oliver

First published in Great Britain in 2002 by
POETRY NOW
Remus House,
Coltsfoot Drive,
Peterborough, PE2 9JX
Telephone (01733) 898101
Fax (01733) 313524

HB ISBN 0 75434 391 X
SB ISBN 0 75434 392 8

FOREWORD

Although we are a nation of poets we are accused of not reading poetry, or buying poetry books. After many years of listening to the incessant gripes of poetry publishers, I can only assume that the books they publish, in general, are books that most people do not want to read.

Poetry should not be obscure, introverted, and as cryptic as a crossword puzzle: it is the poet's duty to reach out and embrace the world.

The world owes the poet nothing and we should not be expected to dig and delve into a rambling discourse searching for some inner meaning.

The reason we write poetry (and almost all of us do) is because we want to communicate: an ideal; an idea; or a specific feeling.

Poetry is as essential in communication, as a letter; a radio; a telephone, and the main criterion for selecting the poems in this anthology is very simple: they communicate.

CONTENTS

A SEA OF DREAMS

Seductive, pure gold sunlight, illuminated the point
Where sea and sky seemed to meet,
As she stood in grimy, blackened waters;
Resting uneasily on silvery pebbles beneath her feet.
A tense, lonely, upright figure, with hands held out as if to clasp,
At a world that seemed beyond her reach, and far out of her grasp.
How she longed to bask in the sunshine, and enjoy a life without a care!
Melancholy and incomplete, the girl gazed fixedly ahead in despair.
Yet one year later, life provided her with all that she had ever dreamed,
A chance to start afresh, and find that place in the sun, or so it seemed,
So she stepped out of the flotsam and jetsam, and completely cast aside,
All the reminders of her previous being with the turning of the tide.
But she failed to hold onto what was worthwhile,
And long-standing in the old,
As she embraced the new, and cast aside silver
For what seemed like gold.
Too arrogant and proud to admit her mistakes,
And reach out for a friend,
Too late, she realised when your dreams come true,
How your whole world can end,
She may fail to recall as I do, that sunlit evening beside the shore,
When she thought she had so little, but infact held so much more.

Mary Carroll

THE TENDER HEART

Beneath the willow boughs
as they weep
a tender heart
gently sleeps

Free from worries
scorn and strife
and all the hassles
of modern life

Sound the bugles
bang the drums
this tired heart
no longer thrums

It will lay beneath
this leafy bower
through winter's storms
that rage and scour

And in the spring
rise with the flowers
but shall cast no eyes
upon their ivory towers

Instead will look
where the willow boughs weep
and perhaps find another tender heart
that gently sleeps.

J W Murison

A NOVEMBER'S POEM

Street lamps streaked across the dark night sky,
Rotating wheels to pass them by.
The moonlight cast upon sullen ground,
All fading smoothly in this mellow sound.

Come back and paint this dark night bright,
With an amber tinge, of urban light.
Create the mood with your designs,
Create our niche to hide from time.

Moving on, we journey far,
A solitude rest, beneath the stars.
Here the dark sky holds the world from sight,
With golden fairies to light it bright.

We lie as fugitives beneath its seas,
On a winter's trail of fallen leaves.
As time lingers with a watchful eye,
A distant tomorrow sleeps close by.

But this frozen scene will slowly dwindle,
With the burning ray of a morning candle.
A sleepy poetry leaves a twisted prose,
To leave by the paths of the falling shadows.

A rising sun on a dark November,
To burn the ash of twilight embers.
The warmth of night has fallen grey
Time has come to claim its prey.

A sombre chorus for a fallen tear,
This forsaken day, we cannot fear.
Reality is unveiled as we bid goodbye,
But memories are sweet, eternal lullabies.

Adele Campbell

WONDER WEBS

Spiders spin September webs
Their strands gleam in the autumn sun.
They weave a span from hedge to earth
With no rest 'til the job is done.

In smaller, more protected form
They decorate my garden gate.
Wrought iron spaces filled with webs
From early morn to night-time late.

Their webs are wondrous fragile things,
Yet strong against the gusting breeze.
Then misty rain turns them to lace
That man can tear with careless ease.

The cunning spider waits awhile,
Then once again a web is spun.
God grant me such tenacity
To finish what I've once begun.

Shirley R Thomas

A BREATH OF LOVE

The Universe sang sweet roses to my ear,
Telling me of the paradise that was opening its doors.
Blindly, I gave my hand.
Wrapping my fingers in the angel's wings.
Trusting the powers would let me float
On the protected cloud,
And not be swallowed by the whirlpool which tantalised my shadow.
The claws dug at my ankles and tugged so viciously
I smacked my face on the stone floor.
Heavenly love was my grip,
Chaining me to the magic gate.
Making absolute promises that you held the cup.
The cup for us both to drink from,
And learn our lessons together.
My tears stabbed me and my child wept.
Your soft hands caressed me
And your eyes told me you were true.
I saw past your devils.
My spirit talks with yours
And my hands dance with your heart.
May our love drip like the life of a succulent fruit,
Bursting with warming potential.

Evie Demosthenous

LIFE

Sometimes life throws at us unexpected fate,
Often to upset us or put us in our place,
The road we pick is up to us,
No one else can ever choose,
Sometimes we may be winners,
Sometimes we may even lose,
The course of life is difficult,
With many ups and downs,
But like the people before us,
We must stand on solid ground,
We must do the things we think are right,
Within our hearts and souls,
And remember the most precious gift,
Is the precious life we hold.

Janet Evans

THE DAY OF SALVATION

So many, many times, you've heard; people speak of me.
Yet somehow, you don't heed their words; those
                                words can set you free.
What you don't realise, is that; the things they say are true.
They've tried in very many ways; to get the message through.
I'm waiting here for your response; I'm knocking at the door
So open up your heart right now, as you I do implore.
It isn't very hard to do; it isn't complicated,
Just say that you accept me, so long for you I've waited.
You've envied those who understand, and wondered why not me.
And said that if I loved you; that I would make it clear.
So often I have called you, it was for you I died.
You just have not responded; but now you must decide.
Will you carry on the way you are, or give your life to me?
Do you want to live in bondage, or do you want to be set free?
Today! make your decision; for now is the time.
Say these words, 'I love you Lord, and truly I am thine.'
Take up your cross and follow me, there may be tears and sorrow
But, for you I guarantee, there'll be a bright tomorrow.

Alison Czajkowski

WHAT HAS LOVE DONE FOR US?

What is it with the word love?
Why is it so special, what has it done for us?
It's caused you grief, it's caused me pain,
So why is love something everyone wants to gain?

Why is it I feel and think so much of you?
When hurting me is all you can do.
I don't want this feeling, I don't want your touch,
But why do I dream about this happening so much?

So please tell me, what should I do?
I've told you so many times I've fallen for you.
It hurts so much, I don't mind walking away,
I just can't bear the thought of you leaving me this way.

Natalie Ellis

GULLS AND CROWS

I heard the sea wind rise
To a low whistling
And went to close it out.
And then I saw the birds -
Crowds of them
Wheeling, crying, circling
Higher, higher.

As I watched
A pattern formed,
Crows and gulls
Moving in different circles,
Crows like ash from a fire,
The gulls curved brackets
High, alone, against the wind
Then turning, gliding.
The crows in gusts
Black swirling leaves
Up high then low.

Were they playing?
I think so
Glorying in their powers
Dicing with the wind
Alive and free.

Fran Barker

WATCHING A FILM

How can I open up,
When I don't know what's around the next corner?
A billboard,
Feeds me information.
In my mind's eye,
I am watching a film in which I am the star,
But when I see my reflection in a mirror,
I am staring into the eyes of a stranger.
Uncertain ground on which I contemplate to tread,
Otherwise known as the future.

Lauren A Evans

ONE FOR SORROW

The leader of the black and white gang
Sprawls, rotting and fly-blown,
In the flotsam and jetsam
Of transient power.

Others' strengths had exploited his weaknesses,
The small, the quick, the alert took flight
While he swaggered and swooped,
Egged on by his black and white henchmen.

Chuckling and chattering with his lackeys,
Strutting his leadership, honing his ferocity,
Preening and grooming his black-green morning suit,
The dominant thug was dressed to kill.

Handsome tyrant, murderer, thief,
Once angel of death to the myopic and slow,
Now devil-black bygone, decaying and fetid,
Overlooked and trampled by an uncaring world.

Tessa Briggs

THINKING BACK

Time is passing by
And I still cry
Thinking of you
And wishing you knew
You meant the world to me
But you just didn't see,
For years I hoped I would see you again
But all my hopes were in vain
Now you will never know
As I guess it is too late to tell you so.
I guess you have a wife
And are happy with your life.
I know my dreams won't come true
And I will never be with you.
Yes, time is passing by
And I still cry
As I think of what might have been
If only you had taken notice of me,
My dreams might have come true
Because I fell in love with you
But I only watched you from afar
Now I often wonder where you are,
So now I can only close my eyes and dream
And think about what might have been.

Eileen Kyte

THOUGHTS OF HOME

Inspired by dreams of youth, I left my home,
To seek the world I'd yearned to see.
So if my luck holds up in these strange lands,
Then I can live my dreams - maybe.
But I get tearful, thinking of my family
And of the mountains, high above my home.
Yet, still my quest in life prevails,
I trek the longest trails,
Though now I dream of Wales.

Long years have passed since I left my home,
So much in life I've seen and done.
But thoughts of home console me, when I'm low,
For those rich times I've had are gone.
I think of her, the girl who once loved me.
Does she still care? Wherever she may be.
Then comes to mind, my mother's tender pride
That day I left her side.
Her tears so hard to hide.

Yet, when I reached these brash and wealthy shores,
Time cooled that youthful urge to roam.
And though there's much to gain from this great land,
I yearn to see the hills of home
And mists in valleys, and walled and winding lanes
The sheep on mountains, the fireside when it rains.
In thought, sometimes, I hear Welsh voices singing,
Then hiraeth sails
The ocean wind, to Wales.

I count the days, for soon I will be leaving
And heading back, to that dear land of Wales.

Gordon Dison

EISTEDDFOD TYDDEWI
(The National Eisteddfod of Wales 2002)

Oh that I could praise
In the language of the bards,
This coast of deep sea mists,
This city so unmarred
By industrial pollution
And the pace of modern life,
A place of tranquil beauty,
A retreat from stress and strife.

This second 'David's City',
This home of Dewi Sant
Was chosen by the faithful
To celebrate 'Cerdd Dant',
And many more expressions
Of their culture and their art,
In the beauty of the language
Of their nation, and their heart.

There many seek the prizes
As they sing and they recite;
Though they come in many sizes,
Yet with one heart unite;
With pens and tongues a-flowing
They seek the Bardic Crown,
Yet only one is going
To win such high renown.

As I walk the field on Wednesday,
Lack of language could me daunt,
Yet I do not feel a stranger,
But the welcome, and the warmth;
The soul of the Welsh nation
Is there in atmosphere,
And I whisper to my Saviour
I'm glad Lord, that I'm here.

Irene Hart

AUTUMN

Mellow marshes now are cold,
Yellow are the grasses old.
Golden leaves soon to be shed,
Crisp the path that footsteps thread.

Cool the autumn morn new born,
Fresh the wind, a coat is worn.
Cries that echo cross the land,
As the day is now at hand.

Ducks fly in and skim the pond,
Quacking, waking up the land.
Heavy dew bends weary heads,
Most of us are in our beds.

Wealth of hues stand out so bright,
The geese pass in formation flight.
Wings of strength I hear them whine,
Long been gone but now's their time.

Puffed is Robin as he hops,
On the branches, round the tops.
For some time he's not been seen,
Don't know really where he's been.

Orange, yellow, red and gold,
A host of brilliance before the old.
Rich in colour, but will it last?
Soon the wind will give a blast.

Berries are of red so bright,
Birds can't wait to have a bite.
So many colours now unfold,
Of falling leaves though some still hold.

Sodden fields this way remain,
The sun is low, here comes the rain.
Fresh, so fresh, the air I breath,
To stay forever, never leave.

Further will the light decline,
But still my favourite is this time.
Precious moments that I spent
Around the marshes, time just went.

Mair Wyn Cratchley

KATIE'S JOURNEY

God had an urgent mission,
He had a secret plan,
He wanted someone special,
So, he gently took your hand,
He said, 'Katie my child, I need you above,
For your family on Earth, we'll leave them your love
I need a child with a heart that's true,
That's why Katie, I've chosen you.'
Katie would have liked to stay,
But the will of God, she wanted to obey,
She didn't know what mission God has planned,
But with complete faith and trust,
She took God's outstretched hand.
Her family on Earth were left to pray,
For a child they loved, who couldn't stay,
We all have asked the reason why?
This special child, had to die.
Each of us has shed many tears,
We will again, through the coming years,
The love of Katie is with us,
It was always meant to stay,
This is our warmth, our comfort,
Until we meet her again one day,
In that far off promised land.
We will know for sure everything was planned,
Because Katie will be the one holding our hand . . .
Welcoming us home . . .

H Doidge

BELIEVE

When sleep comes to claim you, but your mind won't let go,
You're afraid of the future without them, but know,
Your loved ones are only a thought away,
Still close by your side, each and every day,
Those intimate moments - the pain's too hard to bear,
When you turn to their arms and find they're not there,
How can you go on? Two souls no longer one,
Accept they've not left you, then your journey's begun,
The path may be long, you'll not walk it alone,
With each breaking day, you've moved further on,
Glance back at the past to the good times you shared,
Did we take them for granted? Do they know how we cared?
Push these thoughts from your mind, they've no right to be there,
How can we move on if we covet despair?
Stay true to the path whose foundations were laid,
By our loved ones in spirit to show us the way,
How we travel that path, well, that's our choice to make,
Free will is a blessing, don't make the mistake,
Of making the journey in darkness and grief,
Open your hearts and embrace the belief,
As you walk to the sunset where your loved ones will be,
Two souls re-joined, for eternity.

Elaine Nicholas-Chan

THE DRAGON SPEAKS

As down country lanes we wander
trees embrace, their graceful arches
cast their shadows on the stillness
sprinkle sunlight in the silence.
Through the deep and verdant valleys
dappled white with pastoral grazing,
streams and rivulets chattering, chuckling
hurry on their downward journey.
Far away Preseli mountains
rising, falling, undulating
sea of grass and trees, its blue stones
gather in a ring at Stonehenge.
In the dark and blackened valleys
strewn with foundries, mines and slag heaps,
tiny houses tumble, jostling,
men, black-lunged with pitted faces,
men of steel now, scarred and ravaged
mark the heritage of Welshmen,
read their poetry, hear their singing
Pride and hywl - the Dragon speaks.

P Phillips

THE GARDEN BY THE SEA

Penarth, the garden by the sea.
My adopted home, suits me admirably.
There's sea and a prom, but no sand I'm afraid.
A Victorian town, where much money was made
By ship owners, and others, at Penarth Dock
Exporting Welsh coal around the clock.
The dock's now a marina with waterbus and yachts,
The custom house a restaurant, with good food and posh pots.
The pier's still standing, that's Victorian too,
Where there's brass bands, ice creams and an excellent view
Of the Waverley and Balmoral off to North Devon,
Or a daytime cruise on Rivers Wye or Severn.
The climate is warm, and there's plenty of sun.
There's literally something for everyone.

Penarth, Vale of Glamorgan, little Welsh spoken here.
The people are friendly, but the property's dear.
The town's uphill, and the climb keeps you fit.
The park's on the way, where you can sit
And rest, and look back at the sea
Whilst making plans for dinner or tea.
There's a good range of shops, pubs and cafes galore.
It's near to Cardiff, if you want any more.
We're not short of culture with free library and galleries,
Plus concerts and plays, light on pensions and salaries.
Whatever your interest there's a club or society,
Chapels and churches offering choice and variety.
I still like to travel and love to roam free,
But I'll always return to the garden by the sea.

Valerie Catterall

VOICES IN THE NIGHT

I hear mysterious voices in the night.
They come to haunt me.
Sometimes they are soft, gentle voices.
Sometimes they are harsh and grating.
Then I hear your reassuring voice,
'Wake up darling, it's just a dream.'
Just a dream he tells me,
Dreams can't hurt you, only the living can.
Then he gently takes my hand.
'I'm here for you, I'll see you through.'
Morning comes with all its glory.
Birds are singing out their story.
Their song is such a cheerful tune,
For such a lovely day in June.
Dreams are so dark and mysterious in the night.
But in the light of day, they float away.
I am so glad that I have you.
Because I know as always you'll see me through.

Margaret P Thomas

WHAT IF

I lie here thinking, wondering what if.
What if I'd took the earlier train,
Would I have gone home alone in the rain?
What if I'd said yes when I said no?
What if I'd gone out when I stayed in?
There's so many what ifs, where do I begin?
There's so many roads you can choose,
But does what you choose decide if you lose?
Is what happens meant to happen?
Does everything have its own reason?
What if I'd gone out that day?
Instead of leaving it to waste away.
What could have become of that day?
Wondering here I lay.

Katie Davies

POTS AND PANS OF POETRY

Personalities on times clever
on times inconsistent
no scholar, no academia
easy come, easy go.

What matters here
a collection
from nowhere in verse
a simple way with words.

M Hughes

BLESSED WITH SIGHT?

There are so many choices we hold today,
The allowance of freedom of mind,
We choose where to go and whether to stay,
When to be angry and when to be kind.
We pick our circle of friends as well,
What jobs we want to pursue,
Religious beliefs on which to dwell,
Each day we decide what to do.
There are only some times where choices don't stand,
When we cannot change what is fact,
So why *here* is discrimination at hand?
And fairness to others so lacked?
Our colour, our age, our size can be
Attributions which change people's views,
A lot is down to what others see,
Appearances can mean much to lose.
We inherit such genes that create our looks,
Family traits should bring lots of pride,
But like seeing all in a cover of a book
Beneath the skin there's a lot can hide.
It's so unfair that there are barriers to see,
With fixed appearances to blame,
So always remember how boring it would be
If we all looked exactly the same!

Ruth Hutchinson

THE SMART THINKING COW

In the warmth of the evening sun
Beneath some shaded trees
A young cow gives birth
But all is not what it seems
Weak from its turbulent journey
His little legs give way
Onto the ground he slumps
His young life slipping away
In desperation his mother, tenderly nudges, softly moos
Nothing, again and again she tries
What do I do, I could almost hear her cry
Suddenly she turns and walks away
But every step she takes over her shoulder
She'll glance to where her baby lays
As the distance between them widens
She disappears out of sight
What seemed like hours, was minutes, she reappears
Just as dusk begins to shade the light
Behind her the sound of stamping hooves
The loyalty of the dutiful herd
In a language unknown to humans
She'd quickly spread the word
The thundering roar as they race down the field
Surrounding the baby they make a shield
One by one, gently they nudge, then softly moo
Gradually the calf stirs, they'd done what they had to do
Tenderly and very carefully his mother
Removes the afterbirth
Its young life saved by the smart thinking cow
Of our wonderful earth.

Sonia Coneye

AT PORT BANNATYNE

Beauty that changes
Like the colours in a kaleidoscope.
Shades of green -
Tinged by the beams of the sun.

Pine trees like sentinels,
Guard the peaks
In serried ranks of dark green,
Mist cloaks the summit
In a shroud of candyfloss.

The mirrored sky in the clear water
Drifts back and to with the tide.
Crystal waves ripple and lap
On the pebbled beach
Outside this slice of Heaven.

When night cloaks our island
The gentle sounds of oyster catchers
Call across the bay
To the beat of yacht masts.
Stillness fills our ears
And sleep meets our eyes.

Mary Spencer

THE WELSH A LOST FUNCTION PEOPLE

Once Dravidians of the Isles
Took to their own Aryan
Geiriadur Lladin-Cymraeg.
Bust by a Welsh Tudor,
Black death and enlightenment.
Then came something peculiar
Welsh coal and steel,
And above all the Welsh chapel.
Ministers, elders, deacons
And ubiquitous Howell Harris,
With many preacher travellers.
In Ebbw, Brynmawr and Tredegar
On a Friday night
Tough steel workers used
To blacken wives' eyes.
Plonked in front of pulpits
Religion was distrusted.
Future readable poets
Idris, Dylan, joined
Politicians, anarchists, rebels,
Or Marxism in Spain.
Atheism a forlorn whisper
'God is dead',
Reached the valleys.
With McDonald's, Disney,
Shopping mall and moneyed
AMs, councillors: yes
Consequential shelf-lifed,
Flimsy, ugly, houses.
Pits, coal, steel 'are dead'.

In spite of stadia,
Cardiff Bay midges,
The dreadful yack, yack,
Of an inferior assembly,
A lost function people
Who rot their soul.
Dads still booze Friday
In Ebbw, Brynmawr and Tredegar,
Rot their boots?
More
A Dante's iced Satan
Freezes this Dravidian land.

Paul Faulkner

WAVES

Beating, retreating,
Wearing, depleting
The core of the rock
Revealed.
Gravelly, grating,
Never abating,
The beat of the wave
On the shore.

Shimmering, shivering
Swelling,
Gathering resources.
Powerful pressure
Pounding the beach . . .
Stills to a lullaby
Cradling the swell,
Hushed and subdued.

Lapping, rippling,
Saving its strength
For the onslaught.
Every seventh
Is the big one.
Watch it rising
Out at sea
Imminent.

Accelerates, accumulates
Agitates, recreates
Catastrophe
Surfing, surging, running
Ground-swelling trough.
Wrecking, breaking,
'Eternal Father strong to save' -
Never underestimate
The power of the wave.

Muriel Hughes

WINTER NIGHT SNOWFALL

Air, clear as crystal chips of ice,
Jewelled stars on a velvet sky.
Moon, floating, as a lantern, bright.
Lighting up the world from high.

Breath, freezing in the frosty night
Fresh snow, unblemished, covers all.
No footprint yet to mar the sight,
Of this fresh winter's crystal fall.

Moonbeams touching hidden corners.
Whence the shadows fail to find.
A mystery in its outline deepness,
A magic, of a different kind.

Jewelled, star shaped diamonds shine,
Twinkle on the Earth's cold brow.
No tiara glowed so fine,
As this white winter's snowfall now.

Imagination, inspires a thought.
Moonbeams touch the tips of bliss.
Wakens wonders never seen,
A garden, with romantic kiss.

Gwyneth Pritchard

SERENITY

It is the loving kiss - it lingers in the air
    a cradled comfort
        that comes from everywhere

It is the light of love
    that gently fills the skies
It is the dew of peace
    that settles in our eyes

It is the perfect gift
    the present of the now
It makes you *whole* and so *complete*
    belonging so - somehow!

Everything within your reach
Nothing else you need to seek

Quite content you are to *be*
Content
Within eternity
State of being
When we are
Free.

Sylvia

A Message To The Face Of Changing Society

We may not always say the things we should,
When given the chance to say the things we could.
A kind word here, a cheering smile there,
Can make a difference on a face so bare.
Politeness, cheeriness, genuineness not grot,
Alas poor society has gone to pot!
Gone are the days of community spirit,
Nowadays it's all about the 'quick-fix' 'innit'.
Neighbourly love no longer a genuine article,
Everyone scratching for every particle.
'I want this' and 'you want that',
And caring is just a bit of old 'tat'.
Whatever happened to trusted beliefs,
As 'do and be done to', instead of violence and grief.
I may sound like a whinger or even a cynic,
But things seem much better when they are plain and simplistic.
Why be complicated?
Why be complex?
Openness and honesty would reduce some of the vex.
Stand back for a moment, take time out,
No need for guns blazing, to scream and to shout.
We all need to learn from the things we've done wrong,
Admit to our weaknesses, or the agony will go on and on.
At thirty-five I am just in my prime,
I continually look for the good in our time.
So many people, so much ambition and drive,
We should all be just grateful to be so alive!

Lyn M Jones

NEW TO SA19

I have to wait
seeing land greenly
brownly, cloudily white
on black mountains

Others won't wait
slowing at corners
mewing mouthily aahs
at dark mountains

Some carry on
muscle-tyred tractors
spewing petrolly, heave
through steep mountains

What if I wait
tapping out pictures
computer drooling, pierce
the dark mountains?

Carmarthenshire
rolling in privacy
growing greenily, lies
outlined by mountains.

Rosamund Hall

FARMER

He doesn't feel the cold, not he, standing against the bitter blizzard.
Summer took his heart, and led the sun, away.
Away the weary, weary world, turning.
How could death have stalked his Love
and left a world so uniformly grey?
And he a prisoner of Fate,
of passing seasons, sickly promises of spring.
Bound, still, to coax the soft green life from dead grey earth.
He should understand. He knows,
but scorns for thoughts to ease his pain.
His fists, thrust deep in pockets,
close on an ear of corn.
So, he must sow, and reap,
and leave the rest for others,
and that will be his comfort in the end.

Lydia Dier

MUM

Thanks for existing Mum
I know a walk for you is a run,
I admire your courage
I yearn for your strength
You really are the world's best mum,
At times we don't see eye to eye
Although at some point
We make each other smile,
Without you as my mum
How would I survive.
Mum, I love you so much,
Mum, I'm so glad that you're alive.

Paula Natalie Burgess

THE QUIETNESS OF NATURE

You do not hear a snowflake fall,
or the tide turn in ebb and flow.
The clouds in the sky bump
without making a single sound.
Each morning rises the dew
up from below the ground.
This is the silence of God
found only in the natural round.

John Harrold

THE SECRET

Say me a roundalay, sing me a song,
Say we'll be happy, all the year long.
Tell me a secret, a dream we can keep,
And I'll close my eyes and go softly to sleep.

Sing me a madrigal of soft winter winds,
With snowflakes like diamonds and crystals and things,
Tell me a secret that won't make me weep
And I'll drift away on the rivers of sleep.

So dance me a gavotte on feet that have wings,
In the warmth of the summer with all that it brings,
Then tell me your secret before you depart
And I'll keep it safe for you deep in my heart.

Barbara E O'Brien

THE BLESSING

I saw the new moon in a star filled sky
and I felt the wet dew on my naked feet
as I walked up the mountain to the spring.
There reflected in the water was the
moon. So alive and clear that as I put my
hand in the water. The moon became my
hand and the silver light held my heart.

Until like a drunken man I staggered
home. Dancers of this one have to dance
and dance until the blood is strong.

And the dew, the rising blood and the
moon sang into my naked and loving heart.
Worship is a curiously inner
affair with this lover of lovers.

The new moon, the water and the man
I used to be, died and was born
and died again. As I dance this compassion.
Moon scars my hands and waters bless
and heal. What more? Nothing, just dance.

Dei Hughes

LIFE

I'm tired of life, this mortal plane
Where more of loss than ever gain
its hidden rules, its complex winding lanes
Its mired steps and myriad foul games

Oh for a life where there's simplicity of choice
Of knowing where hides truth in silken voice

This life is not as childhood claims
It bends our course, and future, maims

Yes I'm tired of a life that offered more
That tempted me then closed its door

Life is a cruel composer, with winsome ways
And I, a fool, danced to the wild tunes it played.

Life . . . keep its confusion if you must.

Me . . . I'll welcome with blighted heart
Eternal lust.

Geoff Simpson

YESTERDAY AND TODAY

We travel where they feared to tread
Where Gracie lived who sang for them
Or foreign fields beyond their ken
And poppies bloom above the dead.

They never travelled far away
But worked until the light was gone
It never occurred to them anyway
That there existed a foreign dawn.

In ignorance their lives were bliss
Never to imagine this
While we in freedom seek to roam
Their whole world lay in hearth and home.

They'd frown now on how we behave
Our morals would be their disgrace
Perhaps they're turning in their grave
So is the world a better place?

Dismissing thoughts now of the past
Rejecting feelings such as guilt
We decide the die is cast
No more mopping of spilt milk.

While screeching seagulls wheel above
And Artemis now the moon unfurls
We settle for a night of love
No man alone can change the world.

C O Burnell

INNOCENCE LOST

Is it wrong to pat the child - return to it a caring smile -
a knowing wink, a gentle word that makes the fears seem so absurd.
To view in awe as tiny limbs, plod happily over grassy knolls -
cavort in pits of sand with toys and dolls while watchful parents cast
their wary eyes to observers such as me.
Were it not for evil deeds of those who leer and prey on infant form,
leaves me to curse the twisted minds that would rob me of your trust.
No thought of harm pervades my mind as I drink my fill of
                                        childhood past -
immerse my soul in neonate charm - still accusing eyes look on.
Forced by dread I withdraw in haste, the child plays on oblivious,
its innocence intact - though mine is forever - lost.

M M Richards

DID YOU HEAR ME?
(Dedicated to Myra and Bill)

As you stare through a misty view
Did you know that I was there?
Did you hear me say, 'I love you'?

The 'good days' are now so few,
Sometimes life seems so unfair,
As you stare through a misty view.

You're not the one that I once knew,
So handsome, strong and debonair.
Did you hear me say, 'I love you'?

Do you remember me as I remember you?
No glimmer from within to ease my despair,
As you stare through a misty view.

You slowly drift further away - as I pursue,
Withdrawing to another place, unaware.
Did you hear me say, 'I love you'?

Until the end I promise to renew
My vow to stand beside you with loving care,
As you stare through a misty view.
Did you hear me say, 'I love you'?

Polly Davies

THE SLAUGHTER

Wales is the place of beauty,
what's happening all around,
why are they taking our beauties,
the lambs, the sheep and cows.

What will be left of our green valleys?
Is it darkness and gloom?
When the lambs and sheep are slaughtered,
all our animals put to doom!

Our invitations we will lose,
no welcome again to Wales.
For all our green pastures,
and beauty, all taken away.

When we awake in the morning,
our meadows so fresh and green.
The beauty that once surrounded us,
will never again to be seen.

We have the Brecon Beacons,
and all the beauty ahead,
there is no alternative,
nothing, can be put there instead.

So we pray to God for our valleys,
to return for what we have lost,
all the sheep and green pastures,
no matter whatever the cost.

E M Hughes

ABERFAN

The graveyard is peaceful with just a gentle breeze
And the children of disaster seem to whisper
'Don't forget us please'.
There are people who rest with you
They also shared your fate
Many tried to save you
But for all it was too late
No you will never be forgotten
As in your graves you lie
And we ask the same old question, why.
We do not know the answer
And torment can destroy
So we hold onto our memories
Of when you gave us joy
Who picked those precious flowers
And carried them away
I said the Lord, and safe with me they stay
Now your suffering has come to an end.
Wherever you are all our love we send
Your joyful laugh, your lovely smile
You know we miss you all the while
In our hearts and thoughts you will always be
Loved and remembered by all and thee.

Wendy Lynne Bryan

LEAVING HOME

I was there the day they took their vows
Heard them solemnly repeat the thees and thous

Now 12 years on he is up to his neck in elbow grease,
But there are no wages at the end of the week,
And his pockets are filled with betting slips.

Their lives are in pawn and she is crying in the rain.
It is raining outside too, coming down in straight lines
Like the iron bars on the railings outside their home
Which has become her prison.

Autumn has been very sad, she knows they must leave soon,
Is this how leaves are torn from the tree by the wind,
Not yet ready to leave but inevitably they will fall.

The day they left the dead earth was covered
By a shroud of white snow and her small son
Was mourning the loss of his father.

It's now four years since they divorced.
Still no money from the CSA
But a parcel for him has arrived today.
It's a red football shirt from his dad.
This is the best day of his life.

June Lane

THE PITS!

I once was a miner,
Deep, deep underground,
Digging and a-toiling,
For the coal, that we found.
Down in the darkness,
Amongst the smell of damp.
Just me and my shovel
And my trusty Davey lamp.
For I was once a miner,
Deep, deep underground,
Now not for any longer,
For there's no mines to be found.
For now they have all vanished,
Along with all the men,
For I was once a miner,
But never, never again!

Steffan Ap Lloyd

A GLIMPSE INTO THE PAST

Come to Burry Port visit the George
And sample the finest fare
Take in some local history
Whilst you're dining there.

For Amelia memorabilia
This is the place to visit
If you come to Burry Port
Make sure you don't miss it.

In a bar known as the friendship
Amelia's memory survives
It's thanks to Mr Les George
Our Earhart legacy still thrives.

Our restaurateur can show you
Pictures of that famous flight
A flight that ended in our bay
On one summer day so bright.

In the George there is a welcome
That cannot be surpassed
A perfect place to wine and dine
And glimpse into the past.

So if you come to Burry Port
Make sure you don't miss it
For Amelia memorabilia
This is the place to visit.

Marie Horridge

DAWN PIPER

In bedroom-darkness,
the phone sounds reveille.
The byre's a shadow; dawn approaches,
bearing a lighted candle.
Donald waits at the door, oyster-calm, pipe lit,
his smooth morning face reflecting the dawn.

Hay-smell, turnip-smell, dung-smell,
urine-smell; the reek of cows' breath,
the soft sounds of chewing.
Legless from want of calcium,
one groans on her side,
honey-coloured fore-milk
oozing from sagging teats.

A practised thumb locates the jugular, blood
spurts from the needle like claret from a spigot.
Gravity takes over, life-giving calcium flows
from the elevated bottle
into the turgid vein. In mere minutes,
it seems, she has taken to her feet;
the sun's rays reach out
and hap us around.

From a far place
the grace-notes of bagpipes
swarm across the glen
like bees eager for pollen.
We make them welcome
as they engulf us,
and in silence drink in
the new day's first miracle.

Ken Angus

EVERY DAY

Listening kept me alive
the music went off and there I was
so depressed, I felt so stressed
I couldn't even get dressed
but that's just me, my brain's insane
I can't explain
If I could, I would
but I probably shouldn't
anyway I couldn't
even if I tried
I'd blurt out and cry now . . .
I wipe my eyes
I don't wish to die
and that's it
that's the way
nothing to say.
It's the same every day
but not for long
because when I wrote this poem
I was unknown
now I'm known
but I'm still not going
I'm staying for the sake
of every day.

John Scott Harrison

MOTORCADE PASSING

I see the shiny motorcade,
I see the man, the woman.
Each of them hello I bade,
No sign of anything amiss,
A shiny motorcade passing . . .

A man upon a grassy knoll,
A man behind a window,
Even there upon an underpass
No one sees them,
Does no one care?
Why are they there . . .?

I see the shiny motorcade,
I see the man, the woman.
One of them hello I bade,
The other I bade goodbye.
For I see the bullets which came for that king,
I see the toll of sadness that they bring . . .

I cry out, I shout,
No! Don't let them win the fight.
Don't let a thousand days of Camelot
Come to an end . . .

Save your king
Your nation's pride.
Don't let angry men put asunder . . .

I see the motorcade,
No longer shiny, no longer bright.
I also see Camelot has lost its fight.
I no longer see the men on the grassy knoll;
The underpass or at the window,
For they have gone
The chase, there will be none . . .

In blood and tears,
A nation's pride, torn and in tatters.
A lone man found guilty of other's crimes,
Does nothing matter . . ?

I see the king,
He looks so majestic,
For though there's blood all around him,
He knows were it not for that 'shining spot',
There would not be a Camelot . . .

Suzanne Swift

A DISTANT SHORE

I watched the weary travellers land
Saw their footprints in the sand
And there a youth, his face well known
It was the image of my own.

Was this my brother then?

The many years I'd paced this shore
Aye, a thousand times or more
Waiting and praying, for such a day
As this! When I might say.

Are you my brother then?

Memory brings sudden tears
I see again, across the years
The burning roof, the broken door
The Highland home that was no more!

Such inhumanity to man
The Highland clearances began
The Laird, safe in his castle keep
Replacing honest men with sheep

Are you my brother then?
Come, here's my hand.

Helen C Dick

My Land

The heather hills of Scotland beckon now and call,
High the towering mountains reaching grand and tall,
Where the air is pure and life can be serene,
Beauty all around us, forever now is seen.

Silver sands are washed by surging northern seas
Grasses on the dunes sway in cooling breeze,
Islands in the distance melt in summer haze,
Memories keep returning in very many ways.

Highland lochs now shimmer under an azure sky,
Proudly stands the stag, alert, with head held high,
The wild salmon leap as mighty rivers run,
Shiny scales reflecting under a summer sun.

Historic land of legend, music, song and story,
Men have sailed in search of fortune, fame and glory,
Exiles still return as in those days of yore,
To rekindle friendships on their beloved shore.

Alister H Thomson

HOLD OUR PLACE
(PROGRESS OR REGRESS)

Drugs, consider those
Wretches inveigled, addicts who chose
Mad cow disease, brainless blight
Little eaten, processed right
Vegetables, pesticidal versus organic
Apportion diet, do not panic
Old ills, ways gone, advancing new
Brilliant medical progress true
Still Frankenstein boffins casting dreads
Overcrowded hospitals, keep our heads
Surgeons' predilection private, where's hope
Schools over capacity, teachers can't cope
Hygiene yesteryear, less of that
Modern food cartons feed the rat
Manifesting, may threaten plague again
Granted much thankfully retains us sane
Yet terrorism appearing, evil sight
Chilling, hidden menace of darkest night
Life-form, mayhaps, elsewhere in universal space
Of good penchant, would they aid us, hold our place
If evil, to maintain, might we band as one
Face ravening, power hungry foe as we have done
Two hundred years, mankind's colossal leap
To the moon, ending horrors on earth's heap
The world, planets orbiting sun, millions of years
A meteor collision, prehistoric beast disappears
Homo sapiens, thirteen thousand years come
Not three as recounted by some
Awesome eerie history to reflect
Strange awareness earth's hoary old aspect

Practical priorities, are they on course
Opposing, buffeting elemental and human force
Pray we may not regress, horribly, another way
Else man's progress in vain by his own mindless sway

Christina Craig Harkness

CRYING RIVER

Walking across the river
Struggling against the flow,
I want to see you again
As I watch all my tears below.
Listen to this crazy heart of mine
Stranded, I can't get out.
Up to my neck in water
My tears they grow and grow.
How can I make it subside
And breathe the air again.
No more tears to hold me back.
It's you I love in the end
Will you cross the river
And come to the other side?
I want us to be together
Together on that tide.
Baby, baby, don't leave me
I can't take anymore of this.
Drowning in that flowing river
It's you baby I miss.
So will you walk the river
And look for me today,
Look for the crying river
The one that took my tears away.

Niall McManus

REALITY

Something is falling, falling from me
Part of my soul is drifting;
I cannot catch it, it feels so dark,
Cruel images flicker in my eyes
Thoughtless words encave my mind,
Strange tapestries my fingers feel:
Intertwining lace weaving
Images of the subconscious mind.

It's like some abyss that fills my mind:
Reality
And all the horrors of existence,
The dangers.
Tell me, what was so different in the days gone past.
When the Indians ruled America and the Celts ruled my world.
Were things so much better in the times I admire?

When the petals fall from a rose,
Does anyone ever see?
If they opened their eyes would they notice
The suffering the world contains?
Ice can break apart,
Revealing a thousand whispers;
But who would be there to listen to its secrets,
In a society that is today?

Sandra MacLean

TEARS BY THE CLYDE

Alone in my head one mischievous day,
I opened a door and started to play.
But the game of 'What if . . .' Didn't go my way.

I slammed the door shut but 'Too late!' was the cry,
the image was laid out for the sun to dry.
Cracks appeared across faces and the vision grew dark,
I'm suddenly scared as reality is stark.

Up above me the clouds weigh down,
'Where is there peace to wear a frown?'
'No one will see me running away
Or can I fake it for one more day?'

So I hide behind sunglasses and sit by the Clyde,
tears trickling down as I watch the tide.
People walk past and don't look at me twice,
'Why does their life seem so normal and nice?'

One minute I had it and ate it with glee,
next I'm alone and in deep misery.
'Why did I push him to the limit and then more,
Couldn't I have simply barricaded the door?'

Helen Pantony

MEETING YOU (BEAUTIFUL JO)

Springs of anticipation bubbling up inside,
An adrenaline high.
Nerves dancing the jitterbug,
I'm a Twenties night-club in full swing.
Swallowing invisible apprehension.
Scanning faces in the crowd
Looking for recognition.
Impossible, as they pass at the speed of light.
I stand motionless, in another dimension.
Tension, intoxicating suspension.
This thriller far exceeds Hitchcock or Conan Doyle.
Then the wait is over
Beauty glides round the corner,
Floors me as I stand.
A smile that would light the darkest hour.
Shining radiance lifts my spirit,
Offers redemption.
If given the chance,
I would.

Ronald Reid

LONELINESS

I close my eyes when you're not there
The isolation hard to bear
And in the darkness here am I
Watching time just pass me by

I hear the silence, feel the pain
Until I'm in your arms again
Still through the emptiness I sigh
And wish the world just, you and I

Within my heart, and in my soul
Upon your warmth I must console
Reach out my hands for you to hold
To keep me sheltered from the cold

Still when I open up my eyes
I stare out into the deep blue sky
I feel the loneliness subside
As I think of you my love, my life

Marion McGarrigle

Aberdeen Is Changin'

Abirdeen is my delight
Wi' Union Street a lovely sight.
Granite buildings left and right
But Abirdeen is changin'

Rubislaw quarry, once a hill
Grandholm works, was once a mill
St Machar's Cathedral, it's there still
But Abirdeen is changin'

The silver city with sands of gold
Is what we were called in the days of old
It's still a beautiful sight to behold
But Abirdeen is changin'

Changin' nae aye for the best
Some good things hae stood the test
There's little to be said for a' the rest
But Abirdeen is changin'

The silver city with sands of gold
Is what we were called in days of old
It's still a beautiful sight to behold
But Abirdeen is changin'

D K Adam

NOISE POLLUTION

The bus screeches to a stop
as demons pile on in gangs
little lambs dressed as sheep
growling and showing teeth

Rough lingo bitching
bruising tender ears
as shocking renditions
scratch across the mind

A scarlet flush creeps
its way across my cheek
as unshed tears well up
for fallen angels

Escaping from my senses
in plugs pounding melodies
to mask the voices

Nikki

ALI'S BACHELOR PAD

It seems like only yesterday, our first chick left the nest
The time had come to accept, Mother doesn't know best.
Cut the cord, is easy to say, but not so easy to do,
As they pack their bits and pieces, part of us go too.
Ali found a little flat he liked, not very far away
Quite certain this was where he'd like to stay.
As he waved us off, a lonely figure, or so it seemed to us,
We left quickly, trying not to cause any fuss.
As days and weeks passed by, we wondered how things were,
So we telephoned to find out, just what was happening there.
'How about neighbours?' We asked, taking him to task.
'That's strange,' he replied, 'funny you should ask.
The fellow who lives just down along the hall
Keeps banging his head against my room wall.
And the girl who lives downstairs loudly says her prayers
While always outside, scrubbing the stairs.'
'Keep yourself son, to yourself, away from all these types.'
'I do just that, sit in my flat and practise my *bagpipes.*'

Ilean Greig

THE CLEAN SKY

Still under a clean sky speckled white with gulls
the beached hulls lie like rainbow turtles
after the egg-laying. Out on the river
bright yachts glide across dream-laden ferries

in the same slow motion that I remember.
I'm sitting on a bench beside a once-upon-a-time
paddling pond. In the play area is a young boy,
his wind-combed hair and torn wool jumper

stirring easy memories of summers built around this place.
In the cracked depths of the pond, the young boy wades
in liquid air as scraps of paper and empty crisp bags
eddy around him. The wind lifts a piece of paper

and carries it out over the river. Twisting and dipping
like a young gull after trawler-thrown scraps,
the paper dips once too low and is snatched by a passing wave.
I watch as it is carried out to sea, becoming one again with it all.

David Morgan

WIND AND HISS

Sshwaa, sshwaa, sshwaa
All day long and night-time too
the wind farm's blades sshwaa incessantly
providing a trickle of power to the grid
amid the outcry of folk nearby.

There is no need for this intrusion
of sshwaaing blades their efficiency
an illusion in the scientist's mind -
whose inventiveness leaves behind
all thoughts of aural torture.

Awa, awa an sshwaa nae mair
on yonder fell
An' tae hell wi' wun-pooer's
noise pollution.
Hydro-electric dams are
the solution tae aa oor energy problems,
an' ithers tae.

Sshwaa, sshwa, sshw, ssh ss . . .

Bliss!

George Findlay

WHAT IS A MOTHER?

She's a friend indeed
A companion too
A person so wonderful
Related to you

She's a shoulder to cry on
And a helping hand
She gives advice
When things need planned

She's loving and caring
From morning until night
She's always there
To put things right

She's moody like others
But then so am I
Together we argue
And then wonder why

She's special to me
And this is true
She is my mum
No other will do

She's kind and considerate
Her love is so strong
When I am with Mum
Nothing can go wrong

She makes me laugh
And sometimes cry
But together we cope
My mum and I.

Margaret A Hunter

A Border Tale

As I stand at Carter Bar
I cast my gaze so deep and far
Rubers Law, the Eildon Hills
The sparkling Teviot into the Tweed it fills

The River Jed, the rolling dales
Such a place for Border tales
And as my mind transcends through time
I hear the winds through forest whine

The snort of horses in hot pursuit
Their scraggy manes and flying hooves
I hear the sound of the reiver's tongue
A glint of their swords in the morning sun

I see Lord Bothwell, a bloody sight
Wounded in a Border fight
Galloping fast in such plight
To reach the castle at Hermitage

I see our Mary, Queen of Scots
Through the glens on her mare she trots
Across the fords so wide and large
Close followed by her entourage

I hear the cries and the clash of steel
That fateful day at Flodden Field
Deeper into the midst of the past
I see Roman legions on the march

Far from ancient Rome they have come
To reach their fort of Trimontium

And so the present my thoughts return
From all those ancient times unfurled
To write this Border tale.

R E Wharton

SERENITY

Emotion so eroded, makes my being incomplete
Searching for contentment, enormous, immeasurable feat
But deep within my heart, there's hope and faith and prayer
Some day completely without warning, I'll turn and you'll be there

The pain can last a long time, the bitterness can remain,
God bless the strength, belief and faith, that love will eradicate pain.
Once again by life complete, a love to worship and adore
Forgotten is the pain, the tears, the residue of what was before

A precious gift, a partner, to share your joy and happiness
I wait with patience abundant, for you and nothing less.
I'll know you when I see you, and I'll hold your hand in mine
Our hearts will touch each other, bonding for all time.

Love is but a splendour, a feeling that can't compare
At peace, at ease, contented, overwhelmed that you care.
I'll love you now and always, I'll love you eternally,
For in my life you've blessed me with my desired serenity.

Morag Kilpatrick

DUNBLANE WEANS

They went to school that fatal day,
Expecting to work, and maybe to play.
God's little children, the weans of Dunblane,
The world won't forget the horror and pain.

Innocent children denied of being free,
Like wind blowing leaves, newly torn from the trees.

The weans of Dunblane, who died and lived on,
I hope you're now happy, you never did wrong.

Now some have gone, away from our eyes
To some better place, high up in the skies.

To parents and loved ones of those who are gone,
And all who struggled to cope and go on.
In moments of sadness and memories of pain,
Keep sacred the memory of the weans of Dunblane.

Shirley Easton

GLASGOW FOLK

The Glasgow folk are kind;
The best you'll ever find
In the world today.
And why can I say
This with equanimity?
I wasn't born here, you see.
But thirty-five years
Of laughter and tears,
Sharing and caring by
Glaswegians tell me why.
So those of you who hear
Glasgow is all war and beer,
Fish suppers and pies,
Don't listen to the lies.
They will give you their all,
Pick you up when you fall,
Dry your tears when you cry
And joke to raise you high.
So that is why to me
They are like family.

Louise McLennan

MY NORTHERN HOMELAND

Each fall I return again
To my beloved Highland glen
I treasure its infinity
Its beauty and serenity
Each day is filled with pleasure
My Scottish roots I'll treasure
A land so wild and free
That means so much to me.

'Tis my beloved Scotland
This ancient Pictish land
'Tis a nation full of pride
Where many fought and died
A land steeped in history
Full of beauty and mystery
And I thank the Lord above
For this land that I so love

Leaves turn red and gold
Shortly winter will unfold
The frost is really keen
The air so crisp and clean
Deer come down in tow
Ahead of the ascending snow
And high upon a hill
The royal stag stands still

The silvery moon shines bright
Snow-capped peaks glow ghostly white
Above geese fly on by
No mistaking their distant cry
And reflecting across the sky
The Northern Lights blaze high
Shades of green and white
A truly magnificent sight.

Babs M Ward-Schmitz

CURFEW

Streaks of light dance on shadowed walls -
Eerie tremors penetrate and chill.
Haunting silence echoes its own dark song,
As I run the race of life -
By curfew.

Glimmering beads of sweat pour from faces of fear -
Entangled in webs of despair.
Tears fall freely from darting eyes -
Watchful of night, senses heighten - adrenaline flows -
At curfew.

Ray of hope - shine for me -
Lift me from this place of pain.
Carry me on silver wings to the river of peace -
Give me sanctuary -
At curfew.

Margaret Robertson Garrow

COME AND MEET YOUR FAMILY

Well baby, in just eight weeks' time
A strong, over-powering force
Will push you into an unknown adventure,
Squeezing you out from such a soft, warm pouch, so calm
Into the coldness of a harsh and bitter world.
Scared and panicked you may feel at first
Until you hear that familiar voice call softly,
You will cry with all your might, to hear that voice again
Yet so unsure of why?
Heated arms tuck you in gently,
In your mother's arms, you no longer feel distressed
And all becomes calm and clear.
You're placed in someone else's arms,
Strong arms cradle you to their chest,
Your father stands tall and proud as he holds you,
His voice so deep, yet in whisper,
He simply kisses your tender head.
So whether you're my niece or nephew
I'll be here to guide you through,
And your parents will give their lives and soul
To keep you happy, secure and safe.
So whatever happens in your growing life
You'll get 100% honesty, advice and attention
But most of all you're promised 100% love.

Stacey Tully

ANOTHER DAY, ANOTHER SUN

I wish that I were young again
And felt the way I used to feel,
To sense the sun upon my skin
And know that friendship was for real.
Now I am aware that nothing lasts,
That fortune does not smile on me
And we are prisoners of time
Till death does come to set us free.
Yet still I tread the hopeful path,
See beauty oft where there is none
And pray that I will live to see
Another day, another sun.

Rosemary Thomson

MY PLACE IS BEST

From northern Scotland to the south west
Everyone loves their own town the best.
Northern Ireland is unattached,
Down in the south their roofs are thatched.
Scotland, England, Ireland and Wales,
Each and every one has its tales.
What would you say about your place?
Would you compare it to leather or lace?
Is it by the sea or high in the glens?
Do you commute by train or stay to feed the hens?
Does the sun often shine or daily does it rain?
If you could would you choose the same place again?
One thing is clear your roots have been sown
But do you regret they have not fully grown.

Sandra Coyle

A CHOICE

I went into the town to buy me bread
And there I saw a sight that turned my head
A lovely rose - a rose of deepest red
So I bought that lovely flower instead

Though I went hungry for a day
It was but little price to pay
For my heart was light, my spirits gay
As its lovely perfume came my way

H H Steventon

SHADES

Autumn's glories now enfold
Leaves all brittle, red and gold
A whispering breeze filters by
And frosted stars deck the sky
Bracken, fern on lowland hills
Spread russet carpets round the mills
Chuckling waters glisten brightly
While fronds of ice cling on tightly
To stalks and stems that now have died
A new dawn tints the countryside

K K Work

THE GORDON CLAN
(animo non atitia)

Fae the 16th century the Gordons gained their power,
Sir Adam was granted Strathbogie, on that celebrated historic hour.
As the 1700s drew near their strength had significantly grown,
The 'Cock of the North' was how, their mighty chief was known.

Their true enemies were the Douglases who fought hard against royalty,
The Gordons led to their downfall and were praised for their loyalty.
Chronicled is the 4th Duke of Gordon who raised a regiment of
                                                                his own,
The 'Brave Gordon Highlanders' was how they came to be known.

But they did not reign forever, they were outlawed by a royal decree,
The fall of the Gordons was swift as troops plundered their property.
Yet despite the death of their chief and the surrendering of their land,
The Clan lived by the Gaelic dictum of faith - known to all
                                                                as 'Bydand'.

Now in the year 2000 the Gordons are scattered world-wide,
'By courage not cunning' is their motto - it's said with honour
                                                                and pride.
For although the Clan is spread the ties of blood remain,
What must hold true is to remember,

              'the people from whence you came'.

Peter Briggs & Amanda Robb

BRIEF BLOSSOM

Pressed flowers, what stories could they tell
Of far off sunny, summer days and meadows fair,
Of youthful wanderings on hill and dell
Where once we walked and knew not care.

I gaze upon these little mounds of dust
And ponder on the life that once glowed there,
The colours, scents and fragrances that must
Like all life, fade and vanish into air.

Dennis Shepherd

PRESSED FLOWERS

Capturing the beauty of
Summer days gone by,
In a tiny little space,
And pressing Earth's bounty
Into a hand-held bouquet.
Lady's bedstraw, autumn gentian,
Tormentil and Shetland mouse-ear,
Each of these preserved in a
Perfect bunch of ecstasy.

Sophie Anderton

WILD THOUGHTS

The early mist drifts slowly into space
And leaves the silence undisturbed
For just a little while, their heritage is theirs,
The mouse, the worm, the vixen and the bird.

All creatures, happy, busy, unafraid
Revel in this vacuum of peace
For all too soon the joy will turn to dread
When noise and fumes invade their private place.

The road that's being made to skirt the town
Has rent the earth and broken all its shell.
With gay abandon, trees were all chopped down
Their pride and branches shattered, as they fell.

The noble eagle circling high above,
Offended by the sights and sounds he hears,
Longs for the things that he has grown to love,
And worries for his fate in future years.

Carried on the wings of wind, this mighty bird
Alights, and perching on the highest tor,
Safe at last - he bows his noble head
And ponders, and wonders, why! What for!

Peggy Kelso

A BETTER LIFE?

The immigrant ships took the loved ones away,
To a better life so they say.
Letters came back rarely,
Full of hope, then barely
Able to stand reality, they stopped.
'Might as well be dead,
No letters from Heaven
Either,' Mother said.

Anne C Byers

TIME STOOD BY

Watch the clock 'tick-tock',
Time stood by, time stood still,
Have you written your will?
Life will go by with a blink of an eye,
Don't let this be, follow your destiny.
We all play a game,
The Game of Life,
Where we help each other
Through trouble and strife.
So take a stand, be
Tall and strong,
Don't let anyone say you're wrong.
Open the window, open the door,
Don't sit and hide no more.

Claire Farrell

LIFE'S JOURNEY

People young, people old
each human figure untold,
taking on life's challenges
making us grow strong,
example taught upon us
whether it's right or wrong.
We are on this creative journey,
not knowing when it ends.
'Cause life is a lesson,
living each day, facing
all the challenges
that come our way!

Lisa Farrell

THE STREAM OF HEADS

Clear yon stream
That runs today
Totronald springs
To Breacha Bay

Centuries since
Did it run red
By blood of men
Long since dead

The tale is told
That Spaniards came
To rout Macleans
By bloody game

The skirmish raged
From noon till night
Yon hacking fiends
Great grisly sight

Come fighting end
Each bloody head
To tidy tossed
In stream to bed

And ducks did dabble
As stream ran reds
To men of Coll
'The Stream of Heads'.

George Carle

LETTER FROM AUCHTERMUCHTY

Our wee Parliament - take it on trust -
Is progressing quite nicely and must
Soon be finished, although
The expense of the show
Is a general source of disgust.

If the year's been the hottest year ever
Since they started recording the wevver,
Why do so many Scots
All catch colds and not hots
From the sleet lashing down on the hevver?

A fastidious miss in Kirkaldy
Had a really spectacular body
But rejected the youth
Of the town as uncouth
And Raith Rovers' supporters as shoddy.

Aberdeen, that fine city of granite,
Is the haunt of the haddock and gannet.
While eschewing barbarity
It's not famed for its charity.
A donation? Och, sorry, I cannot.

A flamboyant contortionist from Crail
Would curl up in a ball like a snail
Then he'd trumpet with glee,
'Wid ye a' look at me,
Collocatin' ma heid an' ma tail?'

On the night, I saw Scotland score ten
And the boys from Brazil broken men,
And - how's this for a laugh? -
That was just the first half -
Then I woke to reality again.

Norman Bissett

SPRING IN CALLENDAR PARK

Still a dusting of snow on the Ochils
and across the park a steel-sharp wind
cutting through bare trees,
then suddenly into view as though
the artist had stretched his canvas
on the ground - acres of vibrant gold and yellow.
A Wordsworth measure multiplied
again ten thousand times.

Nureyevs and Fonteyns rehearsing
to Earth's orchestral strains
for the grand opening performance,
when every budding ballerina aspires
to front stage status.

A truly magical progression -
this transformation from bud to bloom,
as love does when suddenly
you are aware of its presence.

Agnes Ford

POET'S PURGATORY

You wake in the night -
Pop along to the loo;
Creep back to your bed -
But your brain's wakened too.
You can't switch it off
To get back to sleep
So you're playing with words
Instead of counting sheep.

Various topics
You've not tackled before,
Whiz round in your brain,
Cause a fine old furore.
Your thoughts swiftly leap
From one subject to another,
With no pen in your hand
Remembering's a bother.

A person, an event,
Or a picturesque scene,
Observe, record, who you've met -
Where you've been.
Often your opinions
Will come into play;
As in rhyme your pen
Will have its way.

As you lie there just thinking
Awake in the dark
Each rhyme another
Whole topic may spark.
Your needs must just rise
From your bed and start scribbling
To avoid the frustration
Of lost rhymes that's so niggling.

Deryck Southgate

THE RADIANT SEA AND ME

The energy and fun of the sea
Is there for all to see
The waves move and joyfully break
My soul, it feels awake

Standing, I share in its energy
Changing forms without limits or hindrance
At one with its power and beauty
Entirely embracing me, giving me balance

Before, my smile was a mask
Alone, I receive from the earth
Now in bloom I will move on
Radiant from the unrefined power
Enriched, refreshed and in wonder.

Solvaa Peace

SWEET HARVEST

It's a jam-maker's paradise!
They lie in beds,
Hang on canes and bushes,
Round and red and black;
Awaiting the attack
From the hands of droves
Of folk who come from all the airts
To pick the Perthshire Berries.

In days gone by
The tinkers and the townsfolk came
On foot, by bus or cart.
Locals too, to earn some ready money.
Those summer days were always warm and sunny.
The bairnies took their fill,
Playing in the fields
Among the Perthshire Berries.

Now strawberries and rasps
Must be of even size and shape
To meet the supermarkets' needs.
Now foreign students fit the bill.
(Chosen by growers from the Internet)
As the current climate is so wet;
In polytunnels stretching out for miles,
They pick the Perthshire Berries.

Anne Gwynn

BIRLLIN

Wooden beams hold tight.
Work with all our might.
To build a birllin boat.
To commemorate the past.
Carved with toil and sweat.
We never will forget.
The battles that were fought,
so that independence was sought.
Three hundred years ago.
The clans did not know.
That the day would come.
The election would be run.
Working all together.
In all storms and weather.
To shape the shell of larch.
Beside the boat we'll march,
but not to war my friends.
That has come to an end,
so that peace can come to all.
From Dumfries up to Coll.
Over Scotland, in the Highlands
and all who work the land.
To grow the trees, so then,
we can make the curd and stem.
Admire our workmanship.
Remember the past as it is.
Don't let the memories die.
Let the children ask why,
the birllin was so great
and why the model was made.

Olive Stark

THREE HAIKUS FROM ORKNEY

Gull hovers, wind-borne,
Clean bird with a cold, keen eye,
Side-slips then soars off.

Winter sun blazes,
Pouring molten copper on
The brittle water.

Green thrust through brown earth,
Harbinger of golden wealth,
Year after year. Hope.

D M Anderson

WHISPERS IN THE WIND

Blowing wild like a restless sea.
Gusty winds blindly gone awry,
whistle through the trees.
Haunting sounds that happen by,
Like an all-consuming presence,
whispers in the wind -
stirrring nostalgic memories of echoes from the past,
awakens my heart.

Rustling branches that cannot be stilled,
takes my breath away.
And suddenly I am chilled,
by the whispers in the wind . . .

Agnes L W Berry

PRESSED FLOWERS

Sophie brought her flowers to show,
Flowers she found at Burrastow,
Specially for us both to see,
Pressed and laid so carefully.
Lady's bedstraw, orchis, sedge,
Tormentil from cliff-top edge,
Sneezewort, gentians - each recalls
Memories of her walk to Walls -
And Sophie - may she remember
Summer's brightness next December.

Stella Shepherd

CHILDHOOD

When life decides to leave me and all my time has gone
When I have read the poems and I have sung my song
Just let my memories wander back to yesteryear
Then we were young and happy and seldom shed a tear

We look back to childhood and wonder where it went
The years of youth and innocence so carelessly we spent
Friends from out the past we see in memories they throng
But sadly as the years go by we look and they are gone

Their faces start to fade and dim and disappear with time
And death he starts to claim them those old friends of mine
But maybe in the after years we'll all be the same
Regain our happy childhood and be children once again.

Allan McFadyean

THE WYE RIVER

Restless Vaga, slipping through time with effortless ease,
From high Plynlimon's plain, where wandering sheep may graze,
Your mapped-out destiny etched in eddying swirls,
From fern-filled dripping rocks, to moon-tossed salty seas:
A leaping salmon's shimmering, silvery burst,
Purposefully shapes its vaulting, upward trend,
To shale-encrusted beds, where new-born life is formed,
To turn again, the sea, your restless journey's end.

A curlew calls, crescendo-like in song, haunting the dusk,
An owl swoops out across the widening vale, hunting for prey,
A nightjar rends the silent, brooding night eerily still,
A murky, misty veil slides slowly by, softening all,
Mysterious shadows fill the darkening void, velvety grey,
And a silhouetted nightingale's serenade, salutes the moon.

Norma Rudge

IDAHO WOMAN OF DREAMS

He waits,
marooned in the badlands where the hot wind
scorches his soul.
He listens,
for words of regret,
of sorrow,
just a single word of love
from out of the once upon a time past.
An echo of whispers creeps down the avenue of his mind,
echoes of a summer night when he held her,
and loved her beneath the soft velvet of an Idaho night.
What fear,
what terrors would he have known
had he realised that already
he was making love to a memory,
a fading piece of yesterday's dreams
manufactured by the Idaho woman
with her satchel of dream dust
who came to seed his eyes
but ultimately left him crying.

Alexander K Stubbs

GODFATHER

If I tell you
then I will have to kill you,
you joked when I asked your age
at your birthday party a few years ago.
The number of candles on the cake were a give-away
as you drew your third breath
to extinguish the licking flames
which lit your scarred face like a map.

Our family respected you
behind dark glasses at your funeral;
the sky awash in a green, white, red shade
through different stages of the day.
I heard whispers about your past,
struggling to believe such lies could be true
as my uncles fought over your title and wealth,
greedily arguing over your business;
an unworthy mob.

To me
you were my gentle, grey-haired godfather
who had looked out for me since I was little.
You were a charmer, a gentleman
who kissed both my cheeks when you were unwell
and promised to be inside every cast shadow.
You'd never broken a promise and I believed every word you said
as I made one last sign of the cross
while the priest began to recite from a book at the side of your bed.

Stephen Watt

SUMMER STORM

Racing and chasing and boiling and churning,
The cumulus storm clouds heave into view,
The lowering canopy, spreading and growing,
Killing the sunshine, obscuring the blue.

Breathlessly still is the waiting silence,
Nothing moves in the weird half-light,
Till lightning flares in its eerie brilliance,
Splitting the sky and searing the sight.

Rumbling and grumbling and rolling and crashing,
The thunder a roaring bombardment of sound
Bludgeons the ears and threatens the hearing
Echoing back from the mountains around.

Hissing and flowing and splashing and streaming
Fall fluid sheets of torrential rain.
And away on the skyline, silvery gleaming,
A widening expanse of blue sky shows again.

Olive Cragg

UNBROKEN STREAM

Rhymester of olden times
At rest on a hill undisturbed
Slumbering under the morning star
A long-forgotten voice and face
Invisible in silence
Musing in a much-loved place.

Awakened with the flowers of spring
Sapphire blue-eyed violets
Set in a dew-spangled bed of green
Nature's delicate touch of hope
Stealing through the sleeping earth
In honour of a reborn poet.

Illuminating ways with words
Like fairy flowers pure and white
Bathed in early morning light
Embroidering the wayside of life
Flowering through the centuries
Blooming on and on to eternity.

Gilded winged spirit
Soaring like a silent bird
In the whispering breeze
From the realms of mysticism
Thoughts and feelings
Forever flowering
In a steady unbroken stream
Precious pearls in life's ocean
Vintage of a time long gone.

Beth Izatt Anderson

HERE'S A LETTER FROM YOUR DAD

Kimmy, here's a letter from your dad,
seeing as how I've made you sad,
I'm sorry you hate me as you do,
but Kimmy remember, I love you.
I'm sorry when I make you cry,
every time I do a piece of me may die
the things I do, it's because I am a dad,
and I really know you're not that bad.
To see you cry, to see you sad,
makes me feel a right bad dad.
It's a dad's job to know right and wrong,
but sometimes we do get it wrong.
I hope this smudge on the paper dries,
because it's a tear from your dad's eyes.
I want you to go to bed at night without any fear,
knowing that your dad is near.
I hope your good dreams at night come true,
because you're my little princess, I really do.
You think just now you really hate me, maybe you do,
but deep, deep down, as a dad, you know you love me too.
So when I die as all dads do, remember Kimmy,
I've always loved you.

From your dad

N Marshall

VOCATION

Perhaps you'll sing like Callas, or
Like Beckham bend the ball?
Or would you rather learn to heal
And pain and grief forestall?

Perhaps you'd be creative - build
A business or a house?
Or do you yearn to climb the hill
Among the deer and grouse?

It helps if we remember that
It is not ours to choose;
Our talent is a latent skill
That we are meant to use.

To find the contribution
That we were born to make
Reveals to us the chosen path
Reserved for us to take.

What blessing when we find it:
Our talent we'll employ
In building up community,
Creating love and joy!

Peter Spurgin

A GRANDMOTHER'S LAMENT

Children came with lots of noise, kisses and a hug,
Came to play with all their toys, sitting on my rug.
Children came with gales of laughter and ideas new,
Had a proper spring clean after, many dishes too.
Children came and ate and drank lemonade and cake
Never using spoon nor plate, leaving breadcrumbs in their wake.
They left biscuits on my floor, dirt marks on my walls
Fingerprints on my white doors, papers in the hall -

Now, that they have moved away to another town
Children can no longer play with Grandma's dressing gown.
Now, there's nothing on my floors, neither crumbs nor toy,
Shimmering white are all my doors, but bereft of joy.
Gladly I would sweep the floors, clean the window frame
Open wide my lonely arms - if the children came!

Gertrude Black

OLD TROON

We walked along the beach
In dear Old Troon
We walked the streets
Of the old toon

The air was bracing
The sun shone bright
As we walked along
Everything felt right

We have been coming here
Since I was a boy
To swim in the sea
Is such a joy

Sit in the sun
Eating a snack
This is a place
Where we always come back

Now it's time to go
We will be back soon
To this lovely place
They call 'Old Troon'.

Frank Tonner

TOGETHERNESS

She stood there by his side
Her tears she could not hide
Their marriage vows they had taken
And these would not be forsaken.

He held her hand so tight
Her eyes they shone just like a light
His smile for all the world to see
Filled her heart so full of glee.

Their life they shared and did fulfil
All the wonders of the world.

They sang and danced
And children made
Within their home
They all played.

All those years have passed on by
And now she sits alone to cry.

Happiness she has known
Grief will never make her sad
For she will always remember
The good times that they have had.

J Lanigan

IF ONLY

If only I could see you one more time
Before I go to sleep
Amongst angels heavenly and sublime

The warmth of your smile would me mine
Capturing restful shadows so deep
If only I could see you one more time

As sadly I die and pine
And count lost and lonely sheep
Amongst angels heavenly and sublime

When I haven't got a note or a dime
While dark clouds cry and weep
If only I could see you one more time

Whilst church bells toll and chime
And little birds chirp and cheep
Amongst angels heavenly and sublime

Fairies and pixies dancing on the line
As insects crawl and creep
If only I could see you one more time
Amongst angels heavenly and sublime.

Ann Copland

THE WINDMILL

The rustic old windmll
stands forlorn
down in the meadow
full of corn.

Its working days are since long gone
as it stands bearing
the scars of yesteryears.

Looking bedraggled and dishevelled
paint peeling, timber rotting, bolts rusting,
it is not a pretty sight,
as it fades away by day and by night.

Yet, as if guarding it still
the golden corn dances in the wind non-stop;
around the mill's frail and feeble frame,
until the farmer gathers in his crop.

Henderson Lightbody

THE FAR HORIZON

It is always on the horizon,
Always too far away,
Always just out of reach.
'What is it?' you say.
Paradise on the far horizon
Is the teasing sight.
A mirage of Heaven on Earth,
A trick of the light.

Caroline Carson

ISLE OF THE BLEST

I've travelled afar to distant lands
And sailed on many a sea
But the lovely Isle of South Uist
Will always be home to me.

The shy deer graze on the heather moor
The seagulls swoop on the lonely shore
White clouds gather o'er the lofty ben
Silence steals softly on the hidden glen.

The corn on the machair is ripening fast
Where once cattle roamed in winter's cold blast
But now they return to pastures old
And wandering sheep come back to the fold.

No place on this Earth is fairer
Than this beauteous Isle of the Blest
A far-flung jewel in the ocean
Whose folk are the kindest - and best.

Genevieve Tuke

ON FANCY AND THOUGHT

When the mind is young and the world surrounding
Fills the heart with wonder and admiration,
Sweetly smiling Fancy with mirth abundant
    Sings and rejoices.

Birds and beasts, hills, valleys and winding rivers,
All the joys of art and of books and music,
Smiles of faithful friends and the warmth of kisses,
    All are delightful.

Yet the reign of Fancy is short, and soon harsh
Sombre Thought invades and disturbs the spirit.
Awful doubts, grim questions and dark enigmas
    Gnaw without ceasing.

Free from care sweet Fancy exults, rejoices;
Daring Thought sets out on a bold adventure
Never knowing what may arise to strike him
    Out of the darkness.

Angus Sinclair

FADING GLORY

It's autumn . . . *all right!*
The sky has just been ticked by geese.
Deciduous panorama of ochre and orange,
Sienna and sage, rust and red;
Leaves de-leaf trees
Making skid pans on damp corners.
Dreich mist oozes and cruises
Among rugosa hips and stray brambles
Missed by gleaners.
Salmon pit their brains,
On a scale of greatness,
Against the teeming waterfall.
The grey ghost waits, poised,
Alert-eyed, beak ready,
For strugglers and stragglers,
While the beer-brown burn
Froths its power.
Leap, leap and dash.
Like hopes, they might succeed
In reaching calmer pools,
Before the winter snows.

Susan Grant

SPRING

Out walking,

fragile, pink petals are stinging my face.

Scotland in spring!

Ruth G Hinks

WELCOME TO SCOTLAND

Scotland renowned for its great hospitality,
Nation now ready to grasp opportunity,
Cities and countryside rich in diversity,
Build on the best and make a future
For Scotland.

Scotland so steeped in its culture and history,
Loved for its spaciousness, landscape and pageantry
Moulded by heritage, language and geography,
All combine to make the uniqueness
Of Scotland.

Scotland is waiting if you take the notion
From over the border or over the ocean
To visit a land which stirs the emotion,
There is a welcome here for you
In Scotland.

Scotland is calling, where'er you originate,
Working, retiring, if you want to relocate
You can be sure that Scots will appreciate
With humble pride your compliment paid
To Scotland.

Janet Forrest

THE BALLAD OF DAVY SANDERSON

Davy had a new mistress, with eyes as dark as coal
He adored her, caressed and was proud of her
And in return she possessed his soul.
And as her smoky arms enfolded him like a meek and dutiful wife
Davy was drawn into conspiracy and he almost paid for it with his life.

Jane was the name of his temptress, and a Lady, but not to all
Many had toiled to her whims and desires
But many had suffered a fall.
Not for Jane the fever of passion, just an unbridled lust
She didn't have blood in her being, just pain and the wild coal dust.

Her siren voice called him daily, to dig and to toil at her seam
The sweat that dripped from his dirt-ingrained head
Mixed with the coal that shone in the weak lamp's gleam
He laid his hands on rocks that had been forged by nature's force
Davy saw nothing of the future and how fate would take its course.

But one day Davy and others paid the price that they all
                                             learned to dread
Lady Jane had laughed at their frailty and mocked their mere
                                             mortal stance
Some survived the rock fall; others just lay there dead
As they pulled them up from the shaft, they all looked for
                                             someone to blame
But try as they could, they couldn't just say 'It's the fault of Lady Jane.'

Davy was able at last, to sit in a style in his chair
Useless legs and broken hearts don't make good companions
Nor does the past or the secrets often laid bare.
He'd survived the wickedness of the mysterious Lady Jane
But Davy paid such a high price - he would never work again

Now the cold pit lies silent, her siren's voice is heard no more
There are no miners for her to entice, none to run to her daily call
The coal's gone the way of the fishes - gone far to some foreign shore
So Midlothian lies silent again - sons of the seams, all gone away
No Lady Jane. No Davy - not even another day.

Susan Moreland

REMEMBERING AUGUST

Although it's many years
since Molly died,
The memory remains
crystal-clear.
I can still taste
the smell of fear
and how I cried.

It's half a lifetime
since she died.
Just another day
in the scheme of things.
Yet what deep sorrow
the memory brings
of how I cried.

Remembering that August
when I cried.

Maureen Reynolds

LOST DREAMS

As I float through the golden haze, my mind
Wanders momentarily to days gone
Past. Dreams of happiness lost to a world
Drowning in sadness; thoughts of sunshine
Clouded by shadows; visions of beauty
Shaded by the darkness of things to come.

I come back. The golden haze is no longer
What I travel through. Grey mist forces me
Into a world where I instinctively
Know I do not belong. No laughter or
Smiling visible through my darkened eyes.
I think about home and want to go back.

My new dream does not greet me on my return.
No sound escapes my open lips as I
Begin to question where I am. My eyes
Wander involuntarily around familiar surroundings.
I become aware of the silentness
Of my breathing. I am at last home.

Paula L Roach

SILENCE

Silence speaks volumes
    The tilt of the head
The way of standing -
    Things unsaid

Silence kills confidence,
    Can make us feel small
Say the words - Please -
    Make that call.

Silence leaves others
    Feeling bad
Lost, alone, unhappy -
    - And sad

Silence can make enemies
    - Not friends
Can bring romance
    To an end.

Silence can make you feel
    - Big and strong.

But all alone -
    - When everyone is gone.

Ruth Newlands

THE BOSE*

How come two people
Who have been so intimate
Can love each other
And yet part
With scarcely a word said
And leave them both
Missing the quiet security and satisfaction
That a bose brings.

The risk
Is that opening one's heart
Leaves you vulnerable
Especially when the scar tissue
Is both deep and old
And recent too
And keeping control
Is all you want to do.

For to open one's heart
To a bose
Is like taking the finger
From the dyke
And in an uncertain world
Where little is secure
You need a lot of faith
To hold the flow back.

A 'bose' is a cuddle in local Aberdeen dialect

Stewart McKinlay

Château En Espagne

After you, I'll base my whole life on the foundation of procrastination.
I'll spend my money on cigarettes, never tiring of alcohol abuse.
I'll marry a zillionairess who loves smoking and alcoholics

posing as poets.
I'll 'love' her in a frenzy of apathy and uninvolved self-loathing.
Divorced.
Depressed, I'll live in a cave growing a beard and reading Nietzsche.
I'll emerge with the certainty that shopping is better than philosophy.
I'll become a prophet for *Dolce and Gabbanna*.
I'll refuse job offers and sexual opportunities, but not cigarettes

or Irish whiskey.
I'll move to Spain and build castles on the sand.
Much later, with the aid of Prozac, I'll build prosaic castles in the sky.

J W McKean

PAINTING BY NUMBERS

I've painted my life by numbers.
Been happy or sad when it's time.
The lines were there to guide me,
so everything worked out fine.
Now my Judas hands are shaking,
and my paintbrush won't keep still.
The lines are moving sideways,
and I don't know where to fill.
Someone has mixed up the numbers;
my artwork is getting surreal.
The picture I'm painting is awful,
and I know this can't be real.
I've tried to follow the shade key,
yet it's all just black and red.
There's so many colours neglected,
but they're still inside my head.
I wish I could get a new canvas.
Large and fresh and bright.
With all the numbers in sequence,
so everything works out right.
Till then, I will go on painting,
with my strange two-coloured view.
As to what I'm busy creating?
I really don't have any clue . . .

M M Graham

PEARL OF MACDUFF

I searched for you, my precious,
the lady that I love;
I found you in my heart's berth,
my Pearl of Macduff.

When first I saw your beauty
shine 'neath the sun above,
I knew that you would be mine,
my Pearl of Macduff.

The vision's e'er in my mind,
I see you by the shore;
Behold each gracious movement;
the Pearl, I adore.

I long to be your anchor,
whene'er life's storms are rough,
Your shelter and safe haven,
my Pearl of Macduff.

I'll leave the harbour with you,
upon the morning tide
And sail with you forever
across the ocean wide.

I searched for you, and found you,
the lady that I love;
I found you in my heart's berth,
my Pearl of Macduff!

Ken Millar

AWAKE

Wake up, oh Scotland, wake up!
If you want new life, brother, wake up!
If you want your freedom, rediscover your soul,
If you want to hold your head up and give it your all,
Then wake up, Scotland, wake up!

Wake up, oh Scotland, wake up!
If you want to be free, please wake up!
Fight for your land - not with claymores, guns or grenades,
But with your mind, your words, your friends and your mates.
Wake up, Scotland, wake up!

If you want a future - wake up!
Are your children not worth your efforts today
To build them a future to be proud of?
                    Then say:
Wake up, oh Scotland, wake up!

Wake up and stand up, be counted as Scot.
This is your future in your hands now.
Lift your head up and with it your hand and your heart.
Commit yourself now, today make a start
To wake up and be this old - new Scotland!

Helga Dharmpaul

TENDING TO THE ROSES

Before I lay to rest this tiresome head;
    some words I've just this moment bled . . .

I think that I was eight or nine, or maybe ten; when,
    crying myself to sleep one night,
I heard a whisper tell,
    'It's just a crush, simple infatuation, no more
I promise,
    it will not last, my child,
now, sleep thee well.'

A crush! What is crush?
    Simple infatuation?
Oh, that there were such a thing!
    That these feelings should be so casually dismissed
and not one mention of love dost thou bring; please,
    what of love?
Why not speak of love?

She said,
    'Tis not love, for
we are yet too young for so sordid a business,
    now pray you cease with this tearful lament.'

I still say you were the only girl who could ever make me sigh
    without my throat's consent.

And now I am eighty-nine, or maybe,
    four score and ten,
and;
    as I tend your roses this sombre day,
allow me a whisper tell,
    with this creaking breath
before this, my own death,
    some truths that I've learnt o'er well.

Promises, are fragile comforts
    yet, some promises fracture never;
love?
    We may yet be, still too young for so sordid a business
    but, some crushes, last forever
    some crushes last forever!

A S Loveland

THE WATER GARDEN

The water garden
is flowering now
at the edge
of the dancing burn.
Your resting place is there
among trees and flowers
where the children play
and we all find peace.
So near are you now
so much you understand
after the winter night
with the lights burning in the night
under the stars.

The wild grass was falling
it was high summer
the scent of clover and honeysuckle
drifted in the evening air
and brushed my doorstep
so there was silence
and night surrounded
this place on Earth.

Barbro Pattie

RAPPORT

We have travelled the same road,
    you and I
in a harmony that blends more strongly
    as time passes by.
That indefinable meeting of minds
which defies human explanation.

Together we have gazed at a sunset,
feeling the bonding power of its beauty.
The heights and depths of our lives,
the laughter, joys and sorrows,
hopes, dreams and despair,
we shared in a natural empathy.

Now you are gone, that life-enriching rapport
    is no more.
Numb in my loss, I can recapture our joys
    only in the memory,
in the deep recesses of my mind,
where traces of the past are laid.

A candle has forever been extinguished,
    leaving only darkness.
I still laugh but the laughter echoes in the silence
    and dies in the wind.

Alison M Drever

AT THE CROSSROADS

Now we've met at the crossroads.
Let us sit and talk awhile.
Maybe we both know some stories.
Make us laugh, or at least raise a smile.

And while we're here at the crossroads,
Let us rest and let the world go by,
I'll ease the load from your shoulders,
A hand to hold if you should cry.

If you should walk on down the road,
Think of me as you go,
Guess you know that we will meet again,
Another place, another time.
Yes I know that we will meet again,
As we have met before,
At the crossroads.

But now we're here at the crossroads,
Won't you walk down the lovers' lane,
And if you lay down beside me,
Maybe we'll never part again.

Now we've met at the crossroads,
Have a drink and talk awhile,
Maybe we all know some stories,
Make us laugh, or at least raise a smile.

Clive White

THE KNOCK CRIEFF

I lie in the grasses
And look up at the sky.
I watch the blue Heaven
And clouds floating by.
The sweet scents of summer
Come wafting my way,
I hear a dog Bark
In the far, far away.
In drowsy contentment
I relax on the ground,
Greater bliss and contentment
Will never be found.

Jessica Boak

THE DANGERS OF THE DEEP

That June day bright with cloudless sky
Saw the boats set sail for the fishing trip.
In the wheelhouse snug, the skipper sat
Ordering his craft with skill and hope
Their hearts sang loud as they sped along
Certain they'd win a rich harvest of fish!

The night was black as the hours passed slow
The expectant crew took turns on the watch.
The cry arose with the turbulent waves
'Watch out, my boys! The boat's a-list.'
Like a hopeless cork in the dip of the sea
The ship perched on the wave, then fell on the swell.

Fear, like a vice, gripped the hearts of these fishers once brave
They knew so well the ocean's power.
Life jackets in place, they prayed to their God
Surely he'd save them and bring them to land!

At sunrise next morning, flat calm was returned
But no sign of the ship and no sound from the crew
A dinghy upturned merely sounded the knell
As the radio's bleep dashed the hopes of the town!

'Where are our men-folk?' wailed the widows in grief
'Our children are sobbing.' Their mothers now dread.
The sons of their wombs to the deep they have gone
A dear sacrifice to Neptune, the God of the sea!

The shiny plaque on the church wall clear
Declares to the world the fate of the brave
The cruel sea has claimed them
These young ones we reared.

We mourn them with pride
As we count dear the cost
Of the baskets of fish
Whose dear price they begrudge!

Margaret A Mackenzie

HOT OR COLD?

The winter staggered forth,
Bearing gifts of snow and ice,
The tree laden and bent,
But still withstanding all.

The log cabin shivered,
And shuddered, grey with frost.
The withered, wrinkled occupant
Shovelled a trembling soup-spoon into his mouth.

Alone, physically abandoned,
By family and friends.
'No time for the old ditherer!'
Struggling for his existence.

His family's stone hearts
Colder than the last 60 winters.
Their wish, his death . . .
A small inheritance each.

The man abandoned
By mankind and family.
Happy! Joyous! Surrounded
By a higher warmth!

Stuart McKenzie

THE END

The last word of the world
as it gasps out of breath
our freedom washed up with
the onset of death.
Our years of neglect finally realised,
as the wide world around us
crashes and dies.

Ross Cunningham

SEEDS OF HOPE

He looked at her across the room,
her eyes made his heart go *boom, boom, boom.*
She looked at his tall, muscular physique,
her inner voice sounded, *bleep, bleep, bleep.*
He finally introduced himself to her,
she thanked him so, and offered him a chair.
As they chatted and got to know one another,
he thought she reminded him of his mother.
With him she felt safe and secure,
she believed in her heart *he* was the cure.
They became an item in no time at all,
they felt so confident, they could climb a wall.
Both afraid they'd let each other down,
but, listened to the inner voice sound.
Now there was no *bleep, bleep, bleep,*
instead, together you will reap, reap, reap.
They stayed together and never did part,
he'd always hear that *boom* in his heart.

Anne Keogh

MEMORIES

I really miss the days of old
though they were so long ago,
but in the end like a long lost friend,
they won't come back I know.
The days of school when I broke the rules
whenever I would scheme, the lesson
I'd be taught when I got caught
it all just seems a dream.
The schoolboy fights, the moonlit nights
playing football, the games I played, the friends I made
in days that I recall.
At the dance I'd try to find romance in my teenage years
and sometimes, it worked out fine, but others ended in tears.
I remember the day I got my first pay
I was over the moon
but alas, the years flew by so fast
and I'm getting old too soon.
I wish I could find, a way to rewind
to those days that used to be,
I know I cannot
but I've still got, my happy memories.

Patrick Gormley

MOON SHINE

Moon shines bright into the room
Where once was laughter, now is gloom
Moon shines bright, it doesn't know
Kids mature, they grow and they go.

Moon shines bright upon the walls
Lined with charts, bears and dolls
Moon shines bright upon the bed
Where once they laid their sleepy head.

Moon shines bright upon the floor
Wardrobes, dresser to the door
Moon shines bright, it never dims
I still hear music, jazz and hymns.

Moon shines bright upon my face
Reliving memories, happy days
Moon shines bright, it sees my pain
Knowing life will never be the same.

Moon shines bright, it seems to say
Lift your head, be on your way
Moon shines bright, learned many lessons
That I should count my many blessings.

Daniel P Taggart

PRAY FOR YOUR ENEMIES

Love your enemies, Jesus said, and those who curse you, bless;
And the ones showing you hatred, repay instead with kindness;
Praying for those whose dark trade is wrongfully to abuse,
As they yourselves persecute, and spitefully use.

For, on both the just and unjust, God sends showers of rain,
And, on the good and evil, His sun rises just the same;
So what do we more than others, when we love only those
Who towards ourselves affectionately are disposed?

Yet, when we embrace Jesus' words, we share the Saviour's mind,
And thus exhibit love of a far superior kind,
For what God commands, He enables us to fulfil,
When in faith we desire to obey His revealed will.

But to love and pray for our avowed enemies
Doesn't come naturally, nor is mastered with ease,
Yet God of us ne'er demands an impossible task,
And will give the needed grace, if only we'll ask.

They may fiercely stand against everything we hold dear,
And that Name we so cherish, they in no wise may revere;
Yet, if we pray not for them, there may be none else to care
For their eternal souls and their spiritual welfare.

Who knows, in God's hands, plan and time, we may be instruments
In effecting change in their lives most radical and immense,
As they witness in us a faith that's real and true,
And irresistibly are drawn to trust our Saviour too.

Yes, pray for your enemies, despite their actions and insults,
Believing, in faith, for miraculous results;
And Jesus long ago promised that peacemakers would be blessed,
So pray for your enemies, and trust God for the rest!

Ian Caughey

FOUND ON THE MOUNTAIN

The sheep had heard the Shepherd's call,
That call so loving and dear,
But it went on into the night
With its hopelessness and fear.

It met cruel foes on the mountain paths,
It was wounded, weary and sore,
Then again it heard the Shepherd call
With his pleading voice once more.

But it set its heart on the darkened path,
It continued along that way,
Though its feet were bruised and the wounds had bled,
It looked for a better day.

But it found 'the way of transgressors is hard',
It was fearful in the dark night,
For it had no refuge, no comfort and rest,
And it longed for the morning light.

Soon the mountains were so hard to climb,
And the valleys were so deep,
Yet the Shepherd sought and would not give up
Until He had found His sheep.

Upon His shoulders, His sheep He laid,
His precious treasure that cost
His own Blood to save and redeem
The wandering sheep that was lost.

Are you on the mountains wild and dark?
Have you heard the Shepherd's cry?
Do you feel there is no hope for you?
Friend, the Lord is standing by.

His hand is mighty, His arm is strong,
Don't you hear His call today?
For He is come to seek and to save
The sheep that is gone astray.

Joy Patterson

INSTRUMENTS

The prayers and responses came to a close
And we sat in silent reflection of the life
That had been taken from us.
                    From the balcony
A fiddler touched his bow and cast a reel
Over and among us. The old man's favourite tune?
A memory of happy times gone past?
                    I remember believing
He could hear it still from within his coffin.
And as the bow rolled and strummed
Over the taut-strung, dark-wood fiddle's body
He grasped each note's rise and fall
As he drew them to his heart.
                    The reel ended
And the bow was lowered to the fiddler's side.
Then the silent walk from the church
To the old man's final resting place.
The strain and tug on sinew as he was lowered
Into eternity. Firm handshakes and solemn faces.
                    As I walked
Away I could feel the bow being pressed
Into my hand to take up the tune again.

John Michael Doherty

COBWEBS

The wind of time blows
Through our minds
In each day we live
On a roller coaster ride
Minutes of time stick
In our souls
Just like cobwebs.

A cobweb well spun
With care and attention
Should reflect our effort in life
With a little care and consideration
Not over planting our space
Just safe in the care
In our own little cobweb.

Neil Burns

A FERMANAGH ARTIST

Michael was born an artist,
A talent before he could walk,
An ear for traditional music,
Mick Hoy made the auld fiddle talk.

He sang with ease soft and sweetly,
Irish songs that came from the heart,
Some folks listened and learned,
Others joined in and took part.

A master, a legend, a teacher,
Someone who wanted to share,
Mick left them a fortune,
The words, the history, the air.

He played at Fleadhs over Ireland,
In pubs and out on the street,
His footsteps were light, a gentleman true,
As old friends and new he would greet.

He could tell a humorous story,
With a sly and intelligent wit,
He could make a good story sound better,
When sometimes the truth didn't fit.

In homesteads he played in the corner,
As the turf fire lit up the room,
Head tilted a little in posing, he'd squint and nod,
Sure I'll play you a bit of a tune.

As his cheek caressed that old fiddle,
To him a family loom,
An old saying he often repeated,
The older the fiddle, the sweeter the tune.

The people there gathered were merry,
They'd cheer in laughter and shout,
Placed on the fallen leaf table,
Mick's occasional bottle of stout.

He rang in the year 2000,
Celebrated the new century,
God must have wanted a fiddler,
We had to just let it be.

Music was played by his graveside,
Respect and honour to rest,
Fermanagh's finest fiddle player,
Remembered as one of the best.

Marian McGrath

MEMORIES OF CARRIGOON

The sunny, sunny flowers followed you up the path,
In this beautiful garden there was no wrath.
The front porch was only for strangers,
Everything polished and always smelt new,
It's a pity it was only visited by few.
The sea shells by the side window, waiting to be lifted,
You could hear how lonely the sea was as it rifted.
Apple trees were only climbed upon by the brave,
And under them were strawberries that made us rant and rave.
Gooseberry bushes prickly and green,
Ideal for a place to hide between.
The back gate where Grandad lay over,
With a smile, a wave, a wink or a sigh,
Auld Mick was always there to wave goodbye.
Saturdays were for boiling water,
On the stove from four to seven,
And when Josie got home bathtime was heaven.
Soda farls, currant cakes, buns and wheatens,
Were few of the foods that we had eaten.
The window at the top of the stairs,
Often occupied our prayers,
Under Kitty's pillow we would go,
For silvermints that made us glow.
The one penny jar saved for rainy days,
Was always spent in the sunny rays.
Carrigoon was the place to be,
I don't know about others, but it was heaven to me.

Leigh-Ann Sloan

NOSTALGIA

'Tis time, 'tis time to go about
Those things we do so need
For days away and miles removed
From home our base to leave.

It's summertime, the schools are closed
And books are far away
We dream and yearn for that great sight
Of dunes and sand and sea.

How days are long and sun it shines
We play and swim for hours
No bells are heard, no cross words said
We're in another world.

The weeks they pass, our joy excels
We do not want to know
That some one week and soon perhaps
Our days of play will go.

Then back to home and shorter days
We take on board once more
It's off to school we're sure downcast
Sands and dreams are in the past.

Iris McEvoy

MOTHER
(Dedicated to my mother, Julia McCallen)

This world you carried me into
Not once did you complain
Your passing I now have to
Accept with sorrow and pain

This world I carried you out of
To your final resting place
Happiness I did not have
As the tears ran down my face

Now the world appears empty
And nothing appears to make sense
Sadness it abounds aplenty
As my thoughts turn to past tense

Now that you have departed
And your smile I will see no more
Oh! I am now broken-hearted
And shattered to the core

I know that you watch over me
Helping me deal with my pain
And your beauty I know I will see
When in Heaven we meet once again.

Justin McCallen

TO THE EDGE OF THE WORLD

I dream of
ancient times and
the telling of the Tain.
Stories of wondrous deeds
Cuchulain, Fergus, Grainne and Deirdre.
Swans with voices pure
as water drawn from Bridget's well.
I told you my dreams and
hoped you'd believe
in faeries, goblins and elves
in the Tuatha de Danann and the Sidhe.
Of a spiritual place
a land where life, myth
and legend are one.
Where reality is confined only
by your imagination.
You told me you believed
and also dreamed
of the mystical past, present
future places of enchantment.
Tir-nan-Og.
Now we keep our dreams alive
sustaining them with love.
Until we return
to that spiritual place
our home
at the edge of the World.

Girvin McBride

ULSTER

U nbeatable in its beauty
L and of greenest hue
S oaring Mourne mountains
T he Giant's Causeway too
E veryone is welcome
R elax and enjoy the view.

Helena Henning

STRABANE BRIDGE AT DAWN

The day condenses on the town
Coalescing green and bleeding down
Through beaded air, the bridge
In arcs, and bows around
The river.

All is mist, in fog, asleep
Through which illumination seeps:
A hunting pike
With spectral teeth
Patrolling daybreak, grey and deep
Along blind windows, down mute streets
While the bridge begins to dream.

Under the fading sodium light,
Insect amber-trapped in flight,
Smoke-spanned water, bruised air,
A frozen ghost of liquid nights
That flow away beneath it.

Along with the chimes of pick on stone
And the voices, hammering, blood and bone
Of the bygone men who built it
Block by unacquainted block
Of sun-warmed, dusty, quarried rock.
It floats.

It's made of steam, of cold-breath vapour
It's luminous black words on paper
Fading in the light of day
On its cloudy bed of obsidian sickles
And silent siren elver ripples.
It dreams. It dreams of when it was young.
And I am a raindrop on its back
Waiting for the sun.

Paul McGranaghan

ST FRANCIS OF ASSISI

The sharp edge of the dawn breeze
Cut the stubborn threads of fever.
He woke from the womb of the soul
And greeted the yawning earth.
The wet grass whipped at his feet
As he thrust his praise upon the Lord.
His knees buckled as heightened senses
Tossed on waves of colourful creation.
Fired with the Spirit the young Assessian
Bounded once more into erupting nature.

Brian McCabe

STEADFAST BELFAST

Here I was born, here I have stayed
Known times of joy, times of dread
My suburban home has splendid view
Embracing where old is replaced by new
I see Samson and Goliath, two great cranes
Where I remember the sound of enemy planes
When my dad and I climbed up this hill
To shelter in hedges, terrified still.
As landmines parachuted to the ground
Blasting the shipyard and all around.
Then the colourful dome of the city hall
Resurrects a memory I delight to recall
When thousands gathered there all in clover
To celebrate with joy, the war is over.
The new City Hospital tower block relays
Memories of my daughter's nursing days
I would drive her and my son from the town
When 'trouble' caused a transport breakdown
That also took in the Belfast Telegraph site
Home of the famous 'Ireland's Saturday Night'
Then mother love took the steering wheel
Compensating for lack of nerves of steel.
I see the Belfast Lough caressing the shore
Welcoming home ships and travellers galore
Who still like me cherish the feeling
Adversity has never succeeded in stealing.

Sarah Smeaton

THE QUEST

In what secret cavern lies
The sacred vessel of old
The holy cup of grief,
Distilled through pain.
Tested as gold.

What underground museum
Holds the key?
Dark, forbidding doors,
You hold the distant past
In leather-bound last,
Behind closed doors.

A narrow recess is gateway
To the doors,
Which children guard.
Enter and find the treasure
By which we have for centuries,
Been measured.

The quest of knights of old
To find the chalice made of gold,
Sadly, had they but entered in,
Grief and pain would no longer,
Slumber in the Cold.

To find the chalice
Made of gold,
So the ancient secret will unfold.
Look upon the weeping wall,
And see thereon, in pleated gold and ivory,
And blood-red ruby,
The sacred cup of old.

O Maureen McDaid

THE PROVINCE OF ULSTER

This Province of Ulster which we all love so well.
Has legends and ballads and stories which tell
Of its beauty and grandeur and friendly folks too.
Its history and folklore to mention a few.

The scenery's outstanding, of that we can boast.
Why, just take a trip along the north coast.
Portrush and Portstewart, with their beautiful strands.
Their lovely blue waters and golden, soft sands.

From these northern-most points the view it just thrills.
As there in the distance are the Donegal hills.
Newcastle, Co Down from whence we can see
The mountains of Mourne sweeping down to the sea.

The six counties of Ulster each have their own charms.
With brooks, parks and rivers and picturesque farms.
The land is so green and so fertile it grows
Everything from potatoes to the wild rambling rose.

If it's scenery you're craving and great friendship too.
Just come for a visit, we'll so welcome you.
We'll put on the kettle and talk endlessly
About our wee Province and then have some tea.

We can go to Majorca, to France or to Spain.
But we love our Province in spite of the rain.
So whatever we do, or wherever we roam.
We'll return to our Ulster, the place we call *home*.

Maureen Anderson

THE ANNUAL REGATTA

The highlight of summer in the distant past
Was the regattas on the Lough which flowed so fast
For though Strangford and Portaferry are on opposite sides
Everyone enjoyed the sailing that depended on the tides.

It's hard to know how many yachts entered way back then
With tall masts and canvas blowing in the wind
The starting pistol set them off from either slip or quay
As they set sail up to the bar, close to the Irish Sea.

The yachts back then were owned by lords and ladies of the day
And colonels and majors and people in that way
All with one thing on their mind for to get the gun
And the first prize of the day, whatever to be won.

Then with the onset of the war like every other place
No time for any leisure, not even a boat race
But when it was all over and we had peace once more
The villagers on each side became spectators along the shore.

For the regattas were on again and what a welcome sight
As both the owners and crew mixed well in a sea of white
There were races for every type of yacht as well as punt and boat
So long as it had a sail and able to stay afloat.

The fifteen foot punt and fishing boat was a popular race
For these were sailed by local men, all anxious to get a place
With a shorter course than for the yachts it was plain to see
As everyone cheered and clapped for the winner to be.

Then the rowers in their punts raced across the Lough
It didn't matter if seas were calm or a little rough
There were races for both men and women and mixed as well
With some dressed in fancy clothes, it was really hard to tell.

The gun was given for the winners as the yachts raced back
From Swan Island where the officials stood you could hear the crack
The sailing over for the day it was time to go
To the field for the sports to make a bit of dough.

The finale of regatta day was the dance in the Cuan Hall
With the music by the Hawaiian band loud enough for all
To listen to in the square or on the village green
And everybody saying it was the best day ever seen.

Imelda Fitzsimons

PORTSTEWART

The Neaptide ebbs and flows
Summer rain and winter snows
The crooked graveyard crosses
Denote the town's losses
Of gentle folk laid to rest
The local people remember them at their best
For many a widow's tears can be found
Here where the lashing Atlantic waves abound
As one views on the horizon the powerful hills
It is a long way from its bog peat rills
A seaside town
On a Sunday it puts on its tourist gown
Children mingle
The glistening sea doth tingle
The convent stands majestically on the cliff face
On the promenade shops sell fancy goods and lace
As the church bestows grace for one's soul
Spray rushes up the blow hole
But as one looks four-square to the setting sun
It is time for tired eyes to run.

Finnan Boyle

THE GAME

Barefoot on the shore
The sea rushes towards me
Playing with my feet
The wind circles my body
Swirling its cool, jumpy draught around me
Chasing my skin, cooling on impact
My arms reach above towards the sky
Trying to touch the delicate, soft clouds
The sun shines down
As if defying the breeze, to warm my being
Three elements of nature
Playing with my senses
All have won the game
Elements - three
Me - nil.

Liz Johnston

LENT

Lengthen our days, O Lord
Lengthen our praise
Lengthen the prayers that we pray
and the blessings that we say

Lengthen our patience, Lord
our hope, our joy, our love
and let us long in faith for peace
on Earth as in the Heavens above

Long days of fasting on the Mount
as horrible as Belshazzar's Feast
a miracle of truth is burning
into eyes and hearts and knees

Let us make our pilgrimages
mad across the deserts run
until the Wisdom of the Ages
breaks our sight at setting sun.

David Martin

SWEET MEMORY

I see her -
>Golden hair surrounding gentle face;
>Sweet voice - a sound time never can erase.

I see her -
>Ever watchful of each child she bore,
>Each just as precious as the one before.

I see her -
>When she meets a friend who's sore distressed -
>Comforting, loving, giving of her best.

I see her -
>When so oft bowed down with grief and care -
>All her trials brought to her Lord in prayer.

I see her -
>More dear than father, sister, brother -
>Friend who made me what I am - my *mother.*

Patricia McGavock

ROSE COTTAGE

Long years ago
the sound of children's laughter left this house
The door slammed shut
on many happy memories

This house was lonely
Alone, save for the ravages of time

Around it sprang up briars and choking creepers
Yet somehow, through it all,
erupted roses
pale orange
bright red
engulfing
beautifying

This house was lonely
It is now an object of infinite beauty
No longer alone
but still old
mysterious

Stop and look, on a summer's eve
when the sun shines brightly
on each tiny, crimson petal

What was old has been made new
And it is loved

Helen Craig (13)

LOVE DON'T LIVE HERE ANY MORE

We used to lie in each other's arms,
Our love, it was so strong,
We'd talk, we'd kiss, and we'd make love
Until the break of dawn.
We thought our love would never end,
We'd never be apart;
Until I did a stupid thing
And went and broke her heart.
Now it's all gone because of me
Like driftwood, floating out to sea
Getting further and further from the shore
No!
Love don't live here any more.

David Watton

UNTITLED

On days of grey
the world is wet
    with words
        and memories.

For inside
the ocean of air
    a single sailor sighs silence
and
awaits
the awakened shore.

Gerard McGoran

MEETING MELMOTH AT THE MORGAN

What purpose serve these, the written word?
Would it were that they made no sense.
As it is, they most certainly do, yet there
Still remains the sweet aroma of innocence.

I saw thy life, strewn thither 'pon a wall.
Least, in part, suffice to paint a picture.
Some delighted while others caused unease -
Small tapestries, laid out in chapter.

Personal affairs cause the most public revelations
While title only enhances the disgrace.
And though ally and foe may desert in need,
There is none who could have taken your place.

(May I take liberty to say here
That a literary such as is on view
Seemed naïve as to power of word
And the destruction it can do).

Yet, may I also state my wonderment
On conviction of the heart's desire
To follow, unfaltered and resolute
Though it hailed nought but anger.

A cruel and ungiving world is ours,
We outdo ourselves dealing with matters of the heart.
As a romantic, love shall find a way.
If not, we should stand down. Depart.

As I leave the gates of the Morgan,
I, to myself, swear an oath -
To always pen with great passion
As did you, my dear Melmoth.

Alphonsus O'Flaherty

HAPPY MEMORIES

In winter when it's cold and bleak
My memories of other days I seek.
Then once again I seem to hear
The wondrous song of blackbird clear.
And then I think of summer skies
The laughter in a baby's eyes,
The sunshine sparkling on the sea
All this brings happiness to me.
Dark thoughts of winter disappear
When snowdrops in my mind appear.
My heart feels light, I do declare
I really feel spring's in the air.

Joan McQuoid

ULSTER'S CHILD

'Tis said a child by age of seven
Learns otherwise or to be a child of Heaven.
Accident of birth in Ulster's fair province
Separates, divides, breeds sectarian prejudice.

Generations of bitter tears oft have been shed.
Lives broken, homes shattered, sad hearts have bled.
Politicians, Church leaders - divided, inert
Till violence and murder played so evil a part.

Catholic segregation and Protestant Hegemonies
Seeded the ground for inhuman enmities.
In this sad environment the children mature
God only knows how long this must endure.

Hope came to Ulster with the GF Agreement
But the majority 'for' were too weak and too silent.
Speak out we must 'gainst Paisleyite 'No's'
And the Dissident wreckers each prolonging our woes.

So, children of Ulster - your time to be brave.
Your leaders are failing your future to save.
Break down the barriers of hate and mistrust
And bring to your Ulster a peace that is just.

They say to Sinn Fein, IRA, UVF,
And all those who left their families bereft -
Let friendship and peace in our time be our lot
And erase from fair Ulster the murderous blot.

Let the Assembly be our battleground, not for war
In comradeship and goodwill there strive the more
To bring to our children contentment and peace
Oh, and don't let the arms dumps be a contentious piece.

They will . . . rust
Whilst peace . . . *a must.*

Tom Hewson

LASTING IMPRESSIONS

The familiar sound of the school bell ringing,
Little voices carried by the wind -
Laughing, crying, talking, playing -
At break and at lunchtime,
Then all is still again.

It's the quiet expectancy of pupils learning;
The energy of youth,
Its potential not yet fulfilled.
(Not the silence of bare walls,
empty rooms,
and a deserted playground).

Then there's the coming and going
Of people and cars,
Teachers and parents,
Visitors and friends;
The queue of traffic at 2 and at 3.
The yellow bus in the lay-by;
The line of chattering children
Tripping down the path,
Teacher leading the way;
In spring, their step bordered
By daffodils.

The hustle and bustle of the autumn fayre;
The auctioneer calling,
Fireworks banging,
White elephants selling,
'Three for a pound!'

And Sports Day -
Mums, Dads and toddlers,
Watching and waiting,
Boys and girls cheering,
'Who's first, second, third?'

The blast of the wind
Cutting through the trees.

All this - and more -we knew
As our children grew;
Joys and sorrows,
Pleasures and pain.

These days are (almost) gone now,
But they remain
Etched on our memory
of Sandville,
the school we loved so well.

Caroline Lynch

BITING THE FEEDING HAND

I have spoken more freely with strangers.
Carefully clarifying your criticisms;
You have no voice other than reason.
Who is this person before me?
Slowly, eternally, shaking his head in melancholic modes?
I'm pleased to meet you, sir
I am your daughter;
Listening attentively
For your inaudible love.
I have forgotten if we have ever exchanged smiles.

Joan Corrigan

DISTRACTIONS

Not for a moment will my world
Slow down, for there's nothing all
Around, but distractions.

Pen in hand but no chance to finish
Another perfect stanza, to complete my
Work, nothing but distractions.

To find some place to let my imagination
Flow, there's not a space wherever
I go, only more distractions.

Work unfinished sadness to match,
Writing pad full of nonsense, mind
Confused with distractions.

My heart tells me to give in not
To fight on, there's no place for me
From this hell of distractions.

Now walking in the rain, with
My body submitting to anger and
Pain, wrecked by distractions.

One spot in this vast Earth
Cried out for a bit of peace,
Since birth, only got distractions.

Now lays on the gutter for all time,
Hope vanished, and life jinxed with
Those painful days, of distractions.

Gerald Oliver Sutton

AFTERMATH

The Annihilator came
To our valley.
The wise chose Armageddon.
They would not be
Spent candles flickering,
Gasping and spluttering after life;
And Death found them
Instantly.

We, the fools, wait . . .
A refuge in the disembowelled earth.
Anonymous, stumbling,
Confusion confined
In a subterranean chrysalis.

We are dispersed.
Hirpling lepers, hooded spectres
Where there is no sun or sky,
Where no bird sings or no leaves rustle,
And silence assaults the ears.
Paler greys among the greyness
The shells of buildings are photographic negatives.
And bodies, obscenely grotesque, are
Contortions, crumbling at a touch
To a grey dust
Smooth and fine as flour.

This valley petrified,
Cemetery still,
We do not comprehend.
Meanwhile,
Shuffling, shambling,
Strafed and wrinkled shells
We seek not tomorrow.

Gerry McCusker

Ground Rules For A Wonderful Life!

Don't leave off until tomorrow
What you can do today,
For if you wait and hang about
You miss the chance to have your say!

Greet each new day with a welcome smile
Be kind to those you meet,
For only what you give away
Enriches you along life's way.

Be thankful for the gifts you have
And spare a thought for some,
Who miss the beauty of each day
And wait for better times to come!

Speak your mind with ease to all
Bear no one ill will,
Don't look back on trouble and strife
Take positive steps to improve your life.

See each new day as a blessing
Sent from God above,
A day to work, to wonder at
The abundance of His love.

The time to have your say is now
Let there be no delay,
In song, in prayer and thoughtful verse
Praise Him every day.

Gina Annett

CASTLE WAY

Upward we shall climb
From the meadow below,
Regardless of times
Early morning we know.

Pass the sweet smelling herbs,
In the damp hedges lay,
While the plover circles
In the freshness of day.

The misty light will clear
And is gone like a dream.
We reach yellow sand-dunes
And hear the trickling stream.

We walk along the path,
With many trees ahead,
Bluish flowers and pink ones
Along the way we led.

The dainty pansies fair,
Dewberries and the bramble,
Heather without care
Ground cover to ramble.

We hear the sound of horses' feet,
An early morning rider,
Welcomes the quietness and treat
Of heath and heather for pleasure.

And so we're on Castle Way
To the place we know so well,
While an inshore breeze blows gently
With the fragrant air to dwell.

Ravens perch on the castle walls,
Superior, silent and watchful
Where the archway stands,
Strong and tall.

Travellers were welcome to stay
In ruins now, this castle grey,
Free from banners of cause and king.
For the songs of courage all are gone,
Nature's beauty with us will belong

Mary Cornelius

GIANT'S CAUSEWAY

The wind howled, the billows roared
- the dark clouds gathered and lingered o'er
A seagull hovered above the foam
as great breakers lifted and crashed to their doom.
Moored to a rock was a tiny boat
- heaving and rocking, but keeping afloat:
A family of gulls nested high in a rock
- one flew out bravely to have a look.
Then spreading his wings, launched out with great ease
in search of some food, with the help of the breeze.
I lingered awhile to watch passers-by
and a predator waiting, soaring up high.
Then down, like a parachute, he dropped for his prey
intent on securing his food for the day.
I watched in amazement then lifted my head
to praise my Creator that I had a part
in His plan for a world that was made for man's good
and a God who provided for His creature's food!

Vera Smith

THOUGHTS AND DREAMS OF YOU
(To my only true love, Jennifer)

This cell is not a pretty place
So I close my eyes and see your face,
It has a look of love so true
'Yes my love'
I look at you

For as I've told you times before
The thing they lock is my cell door,
They cannot lock my heart or mind
And I've left this place a thousand times.

I've travelled in my thoughts and dreams
To walk with you past flowing streams,
Then the times that we've held hands
And walked along on golden sands.

Or just to spend the day at home,
To be with you, and not alone.
It's not that hard; it's easy said
But many times my heart has bled.

It's made so hard by all the miles,
I miss your scent, your touch, your smile,
I miss my family, 'Yes that's true'
But what I miss most, 'is you'.

So I'll go my love into my dreams
Of golden beaches and flowing streams.
But remember my love, hard it may be
You're in my thoughts and dreams with me.

David Cummins

SUBMISSIONS INVITED
SOMETHING FOR EVERYONE

POETRY NOW 2003 - Any subject,
any style, any time.

WOMENSWORDS 2003 - Strictly women,
have your say the female way!

STRONGWORDS 2003 - Warning!
Age restriction, must be between 16-24,
opinionated and have strong views.
(Not for the faint-hearted)

All poems no longer than 30 lines.
Always welcome! No fee!
Cash Prizes to be won!

Mark your envelope (eg *Poetry Now) 2003*
Send to:
Forward Press Ltd
Remus House, Coltsfoot Drive,
Peterborough, PE2 9JX

**OVER £10,000 POETRY PRIZES
TO BE WON!**

Judging will take place in October 2003